INTRODUCTION

LANGUAGE AND GRAMMAR

I. The Nature of Language

Language is the expression of thought by means of spoken or written words.

The English word *language* comes (through the French *langue*) from the Latin *lingua,* "the tongue." But the tongue is not the only organ used in speaking. The lips, the teeth, the roof of the mouth, the soft palate (or uvula), the nose, and the vocal chords all help to produce the sounds of which language consists. These various organs make up one delicate and complicated piece of mechanism upon which the breath of the speaker acts like that of a musician upon a clarinet or other wind instrument.

Spoken language, then, is composed of a great variety of sounds made with the vocal organs. A word may consist of one sound (as *Ah!* or *O* or *I*), but most words consist of two or more different sounds (as *go, see, try, finish*). Long or short, however, a word is merely a sign made to express thought.

Thought may be imperfectly expressed by signs made with the head, the hands, etc. Thus, if I grasp a person's arm and point to a dog, he may understand me to ask, "Do you see that dog?" And his nod in reply may stand for "Yes, I see him." But any dialogue carried on in this way must be both fragmentary and uncertain. To express our thoughts fully, freely, and accurately, we must use words,—that is, signs made with the voice. Such voice-signs have had meanings associated with them by custom or tradition, so that their sense is at once understood by all. Their advantage is twofold: they are far more numerous and varied than other signs; and the meanings attached to them are much more definite than those of nods and gestures.

Written words are signs made with the pen to represent and recall to the mind the spoken words (or voice-signs). Written language (that is, composition) must, of necessity, be somewhat fuller than spoken language, as well as more formal and exact. For the reader's understanding is not assisted by the tones of the voice, the changing expressions of the face, and the lively gestures, which help to make spoken language intelligible.

Most words are the signs of definite ideas. Thus, *Charles*, *captain*, *cat*, *mouse*, *bread*, *stone*, *cup*, *ink*, call up images or pictures of persons or things; *strike*, *dive*, *climb*, *dismount*, express particular kinds of action; *green*, *blue*, *careless*, *rocky*, *triangular*, *muscular*, enable us to describe objects with accuracy. Even general terms like *goodness*, *truth*, *courage*, *cowardice*, *generosity*, have sufficiently precise meanings, for they name qualities, or traits of character, with which everybody is familiar.

By the use of such words, even when not combined in groups, we can express our thoughts much more satisfactorily than by mere gestures. The utterance of the single word "Charles!" may signify: "Hullo, Charles! are you here? I am surprised to see you." "Bread!" may suggest to the hearer: "Give me bread! I am very hungry." "Courage!" may be almost equivalent to, "Don't be down-hearted! Your troubles will soon be over."

Language, however, is not confined to the utterance of single words. To express our thoughts we must put words together,—we must combine them into groups; and such groups have settled meanings (just as words have), established (like the meanings of single words) by the customs or habits of the particular language that we are speaking or writing. Further, these groups are not thrown together haphazard. We must construct them in accordance with certain fixed rules. Otherwise we shall fail to express ourselves clearly and acceptably, and we may even succeed in saying the opposite of what we mean.

In constructing these groups (which we call **phrases**, **clauses**, and **sentences**) we have the aid of a large number of short words like *and, if, by, to, in, is, was*, which are very different from the definite and picturesque words that we have just examined. They do not call up distinct images in the mind, and we should find it hard to define any of them. Yet their importance in the expression of thought is clear; for they serve to join other words together, and to show their relation to each other in those groups which make up connected speech.

Thus, "box heavy" conveys some meaning; but "*The* box *is* heavy" is a clear and definite statement. *The* shows that some particular box is meant, and *is* enables us to make an assertion about it. *And*, in "Charles and John are my brothers," indicates that Charles and John are closely connected in my thought, and that what I say of one applies also to the other. *If*, in "If Charles comes, I shall be glad to see him," connects two statements, and shows that one of them is a mere supposition (for Charles may or may not come).

In grouping words, our language has three different ways of indicating their relations: (1) the forms of the words themselves; (2) their order; (3) the use of little words like *and, if, is*, etc.

I. **Change of form.** Words may change their form. Thus the word *boy* becomes *boys* when more than one is meant; *kill* becomes *killed* when past time is referred to; *was* becomes *were* when we are speaking of two or more persons or things; *fast* becomes *faster* when a higher degree of speed is indicated. Such change of form is called **inflection**, and the word is said to be **inflected**.

Inflection is an important means of showing the relations of words in connected speech. In "Henry's racket weighs fourteen ounces," the form *Henry's* shows at once the relation between Henry and the racket,—namely, that Henry owns or possesses it. The word *Henry*, then, may change its form to *Henry's* to indicate ownership or possession.

II. **Order of words.** In "John struck Charles," the way in which the words are arranged shows who it was that struck, and who received the blow. Change the order of words to "Charles struck John," and the meaning is reversed. It is, then, the **order** that shows the relation of *John* to *struck*, and of *struck* to *Charles*.

III. **Use of other words.** Compare the two sentences:

The train *from* Boston has just arrived.
The train *for* Boston has just arrived.

Here *from* and *for* show the relation between the *train* and *Boston*. "The Boston train" might mean either the train *from* Boston or the train *for* Boston. By using *from* or *for* we make the sense unmistakable.

Two matters, then, are of vital importance in language,—the forms of words, and the relations of words. The science which treats of these two matters is called **grammar**.

Inflection is a change in the form of a word indicating some change in its meaning.

The relation in which a word stands to other words in the sentence is called its construction.

Grammar is the science which treats of the forms and the constructions of words.

Syntax is that department of grammar which treats of the constructions of words.

Grammar, then, may be said to concern itself with two main subjects,—inflection and syntax.

English belongs to a family of languages—the Indo-European Family[1]—which is rich in forms of inflection. This richness may be seen in other members of the family,—such as Greek or Latin. The Latin word *homo*, "man," for example, has eight different inflectional forms,—*homo*, "a man"; *hominis*, "of a man"; *homini*, "to a man," and so on. Thus, in Latin, the grammatical construction of a word is, in general, shown by that particular inflectional ending (or termination) which it has in any particular sentence. In the Anglo-Saxon period,[2] English was likewise well furnished with such inflectional endings, though not so abundantly as Latin. Many of these, however, had disappeared by Chaucer's time (1340–1400), and still others have since been lost, so that modern English is one of the least inflected of languages. Such losses are not to be lamented. By due attention to the order of words, and by using *of, to, for, from, in,* and the like, we can express all the relations denoted by the ancient inflections. The gain in simplicity is enormous.

II. Grammar and Usage

Since language is the expression of thought, the rules of grammar agree, in the main, with the laws of thought. In other words, grammar is usually logical,—that is, its rules accord, in general, with the principles of logic, which is the science of exact reasoning.

The rules of grammar, however, do not derive their authority from logic, but from good usage,—that is, from the customs or habits followed by educated speakers and writers. These customs, of course, differ among different nations, and every language has therefore its own stock of peculiar constructions or turns of expression. Such peculiarities are called **idioms**.

Thus, in English we say, "It is I"; but in French the idiom is "C'est moi," which corresponds to "It is me." Many careless speakers of English follow the French idiom in this particular, but their practice has not yet come to be the accepted usage. Hence, though "C'est moi" is correct in French, we must still regard "It is me" as ungrammatical in English. It would, however, become correct if it should ever be adopted by the great majority of educated persons.

Grammar does not enact laws for the conduct of speech. Its business is to ascertain and set forth those customs of language which have the sanction of good usage. If good usage changes, the rules of grammar must change. If two forms or constructions are in good use, the grammarian must admit them both. Occasionally, also, there is room for difference of opinion. These facts, however, do not lessen the authority of grammar in the case of any cultivated language. For in such a language usage is so well settled in almost every particular as to enable the grammarian to say positively what is right and what is wrong. Even in matters of divided usage, it is seldom difficult to determine which of two forms or constructions is preferred by careful writers.

Every language has two standards of usage,—the colloquial and the literary. By "colloquial language," we mean the language of conversation; by "literary language," that employed in literary composition. Everyday colloquial English admits many words, forms, phrases, and constructions that would be out of place in a dignified essay. On the other hand, it is an error in taste to be always "talking like a book." Unpractised speakers and writers should, however, be conservative. They should avoid, even in informal talk, any word or expression that is of doubtful propriety. Only those who know what they are about, can venture to take liberties. It is quite possible to be correct without being stilted or affected.[3]

Every living language is constantly changing. Words, forms, and constructions become **obsolete** (that is, go out of use) and others take their places. Consequently, one often notes in the older English classics, methods of expression which, though formerly correct, are ungrammatical now. Here a twofold caution is necessary. On the one hand, we must not criticise Shakspere or Chaucer for using the English of his own time; but, on the other hand, we must not try to defend our own errors by appealing to ancient usage.

Examples of constructions once in good use, but no longer admissible, are: "the best of the two" (for "the better of the two"); "the most unkindest cut of all"; "There's two or three of us" (for *there are*); "I have forgot the map" (for *forgotten*); "Every one of these letters are in my name" (for *is*); "I think it be" (for *is*).

The language of poetry admits many old words, forms, and constructions that are no longer used in ordinary prose. These are called **archaisms** (that is, ancient expressions). Among the commonest archaisms are *thou, ye, hath, thinkest, doth*. Such forms are also common in prose, in what is known as the **solemn style**, which is modelled, in great part, on the language of the Bible.[4]

In general, it should be remembered that the style which one uses should be appropriate,—that is, it should fit the occasion. A short story and a scientific exposition will differ in style; a familiar letter will naturally shun the formalities of business or legal correspondence. Good style is not a necessary result of grammatical correctness, but without such correctness it is, of course, impossible.

SUMMARY OF GENERAL PRINCIPLES

1. Language is the expression of thought by means of spoken or written words.

2. Words are the signs of ideas.

Spoken words are signs made with the vocal organs; written words are signs made with the pen to represent the spoken words.

The meanings of these signs are settled by custom or tradition in each language.

3. Most words are the signs of definite ideas: as,—*Charles, captain, cat, strike, dive, climb, triangular, careless.*

Other words, of less definite meaning, serve to connect the more definite words and to show their relations to each other in connected speech.

4. In the expression of thought, words are combined into groups called phrases, clauses, and sentences.

5. The relation in which a word stands to other words in the sentence is called its construction.

The construction of English words is shown in three ways: (1) by their form; (2) by their order; (3) by the use of other words like *to, from, is,* etc.

6. Inflection is a change in the form of a word indicating some change in its meaning: as,—*boy, boy's; man, men; drink, drank.*

7. Grammar is the science which treats of the forms and the constructions of words.

Syntax is that department of grammar which treats of the constructions of words.

8. The rules of grammar derive their authority from good usage,—that is, from the customs or habits followed by educated speakers and writers.

THE MEANINGS OF SUBORDINATE CLAUSES

393. Subordinate clauses may be classified not only according to their use as parts of speech, but also, in quite a different way, in accordance with their **various meanings**. These distinctions in idea are of capital importance for the accurate and forcible expression of thought.

394. The variety of meanings which subordinate clauses may express is great, but most of these meanings come under the following heads:—(1) **place** or **time**, (2) **cause**, (3) **concession**, (4) **purpose**, (5) **result**, (6) **condition**, (7) **comparison**,[43] (8) **indirect discourse**, (9) **indirect question**.

The general meaning of the clause is usually indicated by the word which introduces it.

I. CLAUSES OF PLACE AND TIME

395. An adjective or an adverbial clause may express place or time.

I. Adjective Clauses

The house *where the robbery occurred* is No. 14.
The bridge *over which we rode* is in ruins.
There is a point *beyond which you cannot go*.
The day *when* (or *on which*) *I was to sail* arrived at last.
The day *before you came* was rainy.

His terror *while it thundered* was pitiable.

II. Adverbial Clauses

Remain *where I can see you.*
That belongs *where you found it.*
Whithersoever I go, fear dogs my steps.
Whenever the bell rings, you must take down the receiver.
Esmond heard the chimes *as he sat in his own chamber.*
I have lived in Cairo *since my father died.*

396. Adjective clauses of place and time may be introduced by relative pronouns (see examples above).

Adjective and adverbial clauses of place and time may be introduced by relative adverbs. Thus,—

PLACE: where, whence, whither, wherever, whithersoever, wherefrom, whereto, etc.

TIME: when, whenever, while, as, before, after, until, since.

For *as* and *since* in causal clauses, see § 398; for *while* in concessive clauses, see § 399.

397. Clauses of time are sometimes shortened by the omission of the copula and its subject.

When [*he was*] rescued, he was almost dead.
Tom was attacked by cramp *while swimming* across the river.

II. CAUSAL CLAUSES

398. An adverbial clause may express cause.

Causal clauses are introduced by the subordinate conjunctions *because, since, as, inasmuch as,* and sometimes *that.*

> I came home *because I was tired.*
> *As the day was clear,* we decided to climb the mountain.
> *Since you will not relent,* you must take the consequences.
> We were glad *that the wreck was no worse.*
> Tom was delighted *that his friend was safe.*

Since is a preposition or an adverb when it denotes **time**; **as** is an adverb when it denotes **time**. Both *since* and *as* are conjunctions when they express **cause**. For *as* used as a relative pronoun, see § 147.

III. CONCESSIVE CLAUSES

399. An adverbial clause may express concession.

A **concessive clause** is usually introduced by a subordinate conjunction, *though, although,* or *even if.* It **admits** (or concedes) some fact or supposition **in spite of which** the assertion in the main clause is made.

> *Although I do not like his manners,* I respect his character.
> We won the game, *though we expected to lose.*
> *Even if you fail,* you will have gained experience.
> *Even if you were a king,* you would find somebody or something more powerful than yourself.
> *Though he should read books forever,* he would not grow wise.

NOTE. *While* is often used as a weaker or more courteous synonym for *although.*

The main clause, when it follows the concessive clause, may be emphasized by means of *yet, still, nevertheless.*

Although the task was heavy, *yet* his courage never failed. [*Although* and *yet* are correlative conjunctions (§ 369).]

Though his reputation was great at home, *yet* it was greater abroad.

Concessive clauses sometimes omit the copula and its subject.

Though [*he was*] *tired*, he was not disheartened.
This punishment, *though perhaps necessary*, seems rather severe.

400. For the distinction between the indicative and the subjunctive in concessive clauses, see § 279; for that between *should* and *would*, see § 305.

401. A concessive clause may be introduced by the conjunction *as*, or by a relative pronoun or a relative adverb.

{*Whatever* you say, | *Whichever* argument you present, | *However* much you object,} he will carry his point.
Weak as I am, I will make the effort.
Gay as the scene was, 'twas but a dreary place for Mr. Esmond.

NOTE. The adverbial use of *however* is quite distinct from its use as a coördinate conjunction (§ 362).

402. Concession is sometimes expressed by a subjunctive clause without a conjunction to introduce it (§ 281).

Be it ever so humble, there's no place like home.
I will help you, *cost what it may*!

IV–V. CLAUSES OF PURPOSE AND OF RESULT

403. A subordinate clause may express purpose or result.

I. Clauses of Purpose

These men died *that we might live.*

I will take care *that you are not harmed.*

John worked day and night *that the plans might be ready in time.*

We threw our ballast overboard, *so that the airship might clear the treetops.*

All our arrangements have been made with the utmost precision, *in order that the ship may be launched promptly and without accident.*

II. Clauses of Result

He has recovered his strength, *so that he can now work.*

The town stood at the foot of the volcano, *so that every building was destroyed.*

Quentin started *so* suddenly *that he almost dropped his weapon.*

His rancor against the duke was *so* apparent *that one saw it in the first half-hour's conversation.*

Their minds were *so* much embittered *that they imputed to each other nothing less than deliberate villany.*

You make *such* a noise *that I cannot hear the music.*

404. Clauses of purpose may be introduced by the subordinate conjunction *that* or by a phrase containing it (*so that, in order that, to the end that,* etc.).

Negative clauses of purpose may be introduced by *that ... not* or by *lest*. For *lest* with the subjunctive, see § 284.

> Take heed *lest thou fall.*
> I feared *lest I might anger thee.*—SHAKSPERE.

405. Clauses of result may be introduced by the phrase *so that*, consisting of the adverb *so* and the subordinate conjunction *that*; or by *that* alone, especially when *so, such,* or some similar word stands in the main clause.

406. A clause of **purpose** or of **result** may be either an **adverbial clause** (as in § 403) or a **substantive clause**.

> I intend *that you shall be elected.* [Object.]
> My intention is *that you shall be appointed.* [Predicate nominative.]
> The result is *that he is bankrupt.* [Predicate nominative.]
> His exertions had this effect, *that the vote was unanimous.* [Appositive.]

407. A substantive clause of purpose is often used as the **object** of a verb of *commanding, desiring,* or the like.

> The general ordered *that the fort should be blown up.*
> The prisoner begged *that his fetters might be struck off.*

408. For subordinate clauses with *shall* or *should*, implying purpose or expectation, see § 304.

409. Purpose may be expressed by the infinitive with *to* or *in order to*, and result by the infinitive with *to* or *as to*.

He abandoned his profession *to* [or *in order to*] *become a missionary*. [Purpose.]

He was kind enough *to help me*. [Result. Compare: He was so kind *that he helped me*.]

He was so kind *as to help me*. [Result.]

Negative result is often expressed by the adverb *too* and the infinitive.

Iron is *too* heavy *to float*. [Compare: Iron is so heavy *that it does not float*.]

410. Purpose may be expressed by an **infinitive clause** (§ 325).

The teacher intended *us to finish the book*. [Compare: The teacher intended *that we should finish the book*.]

The foreman ordered *the engine to be stopped*. [Compare: The foreman ordered *that the engine should be stopped*.]

VI. CONDITIONAL SENTENCES

411. A clause that expresses a condition introduced by *if*, or by some equivalent word or phrase, is called a conditional clause.

A sentence that contains a conditional clause is called a conditional sentence.

If it rains, we shall remain at home.
I shall attend the convention *if I am in town*.
I will take this book, *if you please*.

412. A *conditional sentence* in its simplest form consists of two parts:—
(1) A subordinate (adverbial) clause, commonly introduced by *if*, and expressing the **condition**.

(2) A main clause expressing the **conclusion**, that is, the statement which is true in case the condition expressed in the *if*-clause is true.

> Thus in the first example in § 411, the **condition** is *if it rains*; the **conclusion** is *we shall remain at home*.

Either the condition or the conclusion may come first.

> The conditional clause is often called the **protasis**, and the conclusion is often called the **apodosis**.

The **conclusion** of a conditional sentence may be declarative, interrogative, imperative, or exclamatory.

> If you go to Philadelphia, *where shall you stay*? [Interrogative.]
> *Sit here*, if you wish. [Imperative.]
> If you win the prize, *how glad I shall be*! [Exclamatory.]

413. A conditional clause may be introduced by *provided* (or *provided that*), *granted that*, *supposing* (or *suppose*), *on condition that*.

> I will permit you to go, *on condition that* you come home early.
> You may have the money, *provided* you will put it in the bank.
> *Supposing* (or *suppose*) it rains, what shall we do?

> *Suppose* is really an imperative and *supposing* a participle, the clause being the object.

414. A **negative condition** is commonly introduced by *if ... not* or *unless*.

> I will wait for him, *if* you do *not* object.
> *Unless* you overcome that habit, you will be ruined.

415. Double (or **alternative**) **conditions** may be introduced by *whether ... or*.

Whether he goes or stays, he must pay a week's board.
[Compare: *If* he goes *or if* he stays, etc.]

He is determined to buy that car, *whether* you approve *or* not.
[That is: *if* you approve *or if* you do not approve.]

416. A conditional clause may be introduced by *whoever, whenever,* or some similar compound (§§ 159, 195).

Whoever offends, is punished. [Compare: *If anybody* offends, he is punished.]

Whoever shall offend, shall be punished.

Whomever you ask, you will be disappointed. [Compare: If you shall ask anybody.]

He will come *whenever* [= *if ever*] he is called.

NOTE. In older English and in poetry, *who* is common in this construction: as,—"*Who* [= *whoever*] steals my purse, steals trash" (SHAKSPERE).

417. A conditional clause sometimes omits the copula and its subject.

I will go if [*it is*] necessary.
If [*it is*] possible, come to-morrow.

The *if*-clause is sometimes used as an exclamation, with the conclusion omitted.

If I only had a rifle!

418. A condition may be expressed by means of an assertion, a question, an imperative, or the absolute construction (§ 345).

We take the receiver from the hook, and the operator answers.
We replace it, and the connection is broken. [Compare: If we take

the receiver from the hook, the operator answers, etc.]

> Press that button, and the bell will ring.
> Do you refuse? Then you must take the consequences.
> We shall sail on Monday, weather permitting.

NOTE. In such cases, there is no subordinate conditional clause. Thus, in the first example, we have two independent coördinate clauses, making a compound sentence (§ 44).

FORMS OF CONDITIONS

419. Conditional sentences show great variety of form, but it is easy to classify them according to the **time** of the supposed case and the **degree of doubt** that the speaker expresses.

420. Conditions may be **present**, **past**, or **future**.

PRESENT AND PAST CONDITIONS

421. Present and past conditions may be either (1) **non-committal** or (2) **contrary to fact**.

1. A condition is **non-committal** when it implies nothing as to the truth or falsity of the case supposed.

> *If James is angry,* I am sorry. [Perhaps James is angry, perhaps not.]

2. A condition is **contrary to fact** when it implies that the supposed case is not or was not true.

> *If James were angry,* I should be sorry. [James is *not* angry.]

422. In a **non-committal present condition**, the *if*-clause[44] takes the present indicative; in a **non-committal past condition**, the past, the perfect, or the pluperfect.

The conclusion may be in any form that the sense allows.

I. Present Condition, Non-committal

If this pebble is a diamond, {it is valuable. | guard it carefully. | you have made a great discovery. | you will get a large sum for it. | why are you so careless of it? | what a prize it is!}

If it is raining, shut the window.

If Jack lives in this house, {he is a lucky boy. | ring the bell. | he has moved since last May.}

II. Past Condition, Non-committal

If that pebble was a diamond, {it was valuable. | why did you throw it away? | go back and look for it.}

If Tom has apologized, {he has done his duty. | you ought to excuse him. | forgive him.}

If John had reached home before we started, he must have made a quick journey.

In each of these examples, the speaker declines to commit himself as to the truth of the supposed case. Perhaps the pebble was a diamond, perhaps not; Tom may or may not have apologized; whether or not John had reached home, we cannot tell.

423. In a **condition contrary to fact**, the *if*-clause takes the past subjunctive when the condition refers to present time, the pluperfect subjunctive when it refers to past time.

The conclusion regularly takes *should* or *would* (§ 286, 3).

If John *were* here, I *should recognize* him. [Present condition, present conclusion.]

If John *were* here, I *should have recognized* him before this. [Present condition, past conclusion.]

If I *had offended* him, I *should have regretted* it. [Past condition, past conclusion.]

If I *had* then *offended* him, I *should regret* it now. [Past condition, present conclusion.]

In each of these sentences, the speaker distinctly implies that the supposed case (or **condition**) *is* (or *was*) *not a fact*. It follows, of course, that the **conclusion** is not a fact:—John is *not* here; therefore I *do not* recognize him.

424. In conditions contrary to fact, the subjunctive without *if* is common. In this use, the subject follows the verb (§ 281).

Were he my friend, I should *expect* his help. [= If he *were* my friend. Present condition, contrary to fact.]

Had he *been* my friend, I should have *expected* his help. [= If he *had been* my friend. Past condition, contrary to fact.]

NOTE. In older English, the subjunctive may be used in both clauses: as,—"He *were* no lion, *were* not Romans hinds" (SHAKSPERE).

Future Conditions

425. Future conditions always imply **doubt**, for no one can tell what may or may not happen to-morrow.

426. In all future conditions, some verb-form denoting future time is used in both clauses.

1. In a future condition which suggests nothing as to the probability or improbability of the case supposed, the present indicative is regularly used in the *if*-clause, and the future indicative in the conclusion.

> If it *rains* to-morrow, I *shall* not *go*.

In very formal or exact language a verb-phrase with *shall* may be used in the *if*-clause: as,—"If it *shall rain* to-morrow, I shall not go."

2. The present subjunctive is sometimes used in the *if*-clause. This form commonly suggests more doubt than the present indicative.

> If it *rain* to-morrow, I shall not go.

3. In a future condition which puts the supposed case rather vaguely, often with a considerable suggestion of doubt, a verb-phrase with *should* or *would* is used in both clauses.

> If it *should rain* to-morrow, I *should* not *go*.

For the use of *should* or *would* in such clauses, see § 305.

A phrase with *were to* may replace the *should*-phrase in the *if*-clause. This form often emphasizes the suggestion of doubt.

> If it *were to rain* to-morrow, I should not go.

The past subjunctive may stand in the *if*-clause instead of the *should*-phrase.

> If it *rained* to-morrow, I should not go.

NOTE. The comparative amount of doubt implied in the different kinds of future conditions cannot be defined with precision; for it varies with the circumstances or the context, and often depends on emphasis or the tone of the voice. Thus, in "if it should rain to-morrow," *should* may be so emphasized as to make the supposed case seem highly improbable, whereas an emphasis on *to-morrow* would have a very different effect. As to the subjunctive, its use is often due rather to the writer's liking for that mood than to any special doubt in his mind.

427. For *even if* in concessive clauses, see § 399; for *as if* in clauses of comparison, see § 428; for *if* (in the sense of *whether*) in indirect questions, see § 442.

VII. CLAUSES OF COMPARISON

428. An adverbial clause introduced by *as if* may express comparison.[45]

> You speak *as if you were angry.*[46]
> He breathes *as if he were exhausted.*
> She cared for me *as if I had been her son.*

As though is also used, but *as if* is now preferred by most writers.

The subjunctive *were*, not the indicative *was*, is used after *as if* (§ 282).

429. *As* and *than*, as subordinate conjunctions, introduce **clauses of comparison** or **degree**.

> You are as old *as he* [*is*].
> I am younger *than you* [*are*].
> He weighs as much *as I* [*weigh*].
> I pity you more *than* [*I pity*] *her.*

When the verb is omitted, the substantive that follows *as* or *than* is in the same case in which it would stand if the verb were expressed. Thus,—

> You are stronger than *he*. [Not: than *him*.]
> I see you oftener than *him*. [Not: than *he*.]
> He plays a better game than *I*. [Not: than *me*.]

They will miss John more than *me*. [That is: more than they miss *me*.]

VIII. INDIRECT DISCOURSE

430. A quotation may be **direct** or **indirect**.

A **direct quotation** repeats a speech or thought in its original form.

> I replied: "I am sorry to hear it."
> "Henceforth," he explained, "I shall call on Tuesdays."
> "You must see California," she insisted.
> "Elizabeth no longer lives here," he said.
> "I know nothing about it," was the witness's reply.
> "Where," thought I, "are the crew?"[47]

An **indirect quotation** repeats a speech or thought in substance, but usually with some change in its form.

An indirect quotation, when a statement, is a subordinate clause dependent on some word of *saying* or *thinking*, and introduced by the conjunction *that*.

> I replied *that I was sorry to hear it*. [Direct: I am sorry.]
> He explained *that henceforth he should call on Tuesdays*.
> She insisted *that I must see California*.

A direct quotation begins with a **capital letter**, unless it is a fragment of a sentence. It is enclosed in **quotation marks**.

An indirect quotation begins with a **small letter**. It usually has no quotation marks.

431. A substantive clause introduced by *that* **may be used with verbs and other expressions of** *telling, thinking, knowing,* **and** *perceiving,* **to**

report the words or thought of a person in substance, but usually with some change of form.

Such clauses are said to be in the indirect discourse.

> For distinction, a remark or a thought in its original form (as in a direct quotation) is said to be in the **direct discourse**.

432. Statements in *indirect discourse*, being substantive clauses, may be used in various noun constructions: (1) as **object** of some verb of *telling*, *thinking*, or the like, (2) as **subject**, (3) as **predicate nominative**, (4) as **appositive**.

> He said *that the box was empty*. [Object.]
>
> *That the box was empty* was all he could say. [Subject.]
>
> My remark was *that the bill is a menace*. [Predicate nominative.]
>
> Your remark, *that the bill is a menace*, has aroused vigorous protest. [Apposition.]

433. The conjunction *that* is often omitted.

> Jack said [*that*] he was sorry.
>
> I hope [*that*] you can come.
>
> I know he is too busy a man to have leisure for me.—Cowper.

434. In indirect discourse, after the past or the pluperfect tense, the present tense of the direct discourse becomes past, and the perfect becomes pluperfect.

> 1. Direct: I *am* tired.
>
> Indirect: John {said | had said} that he *was* tired.
>
> 2. Direct: I *have won*.

INDIRECT: John {said | had said} that he *had won*.

But a general or universal truth always remains in the present tense.

DIRECT: Air *is* a gas.
INDIRECT: I told him that air *is* a gas.
INDIRECT: I had told him a hundred times that air *is* a gas.

435. The clause with *that* in indirect discourse is sometimes replaced by an infinitive clause (§ 325).

The jury declared *him to be innocent*. [Compare: The jury declared *that he was innocent*.]

Morton admitted *them to be counterfeit*. [Compare: Morton admitted *that they were counterfeit*.]

In these sentences, *him* and *them* are, of course, the subjects of the infinitives, not the objects of *declared* and *admitted*.

436. When the verb of *telling* or *thinking* is in the **passive voice**, three constructions occur:—

1. A clause with *that* is used as the subject of the passive verb.

That Rogers desires the office is commonly reported.

2. The expletive *it* is used as the grammatical subject, and a *that*-clause follows the passive verb.

It is commonly reported that Rogers desires the office.

3. The subject of the *that*-clause becomes the subject of the passive verb, and the verb of the clause is replaced by an infinitive.

Rogers is commonly reported to desire the office.

The choice among these three idioms is largely a matter of emphasis or euphony. The first may easily become heavy or awkward, and it is therefore less common than either of the others.

> NOTE. The third of these idioms is often called the **personal construction**, to distinguish it from the second, in which the grammatical subject is the impersonal *it* (§ 120, 1). The infinitive in this third idiom may be regarded as a peculiar adverbial modifier of the passive verb.

Further examples of the three constructions with passive verbs of *telling*, *thinking*, etc., are the following:—

> That in vivacity, humor, and eloquence, the Irish stand high among the nations of the world is now universally acknowledged.—MACAULAY.
>
> It is admitted that the exercise of the imagination is most delightful.—SHELLEY.
>
> It must be owned that Charles's life has points of some originality.—STEVENSON.
>
> Porto Bello is still said to be impregnable, and it is reported the Dutch have declared war against us.—GRAY.
>
> He was generally believed to have been a pirate.—LYTTON.
>
> Pope may be said to write always with his reputation in his head.—JOHNSON.
>
> She was observed to flutter her fan with such vehement rapidity that the elaborate delicacy of its workmanship gave way.—HAWTHORNE.
>
> This is said to be the only château in France in which the ancient furniture of its original age is preserved.—LONGFELLOW.

437. A substantive clause with *that* is common after *it seems, it is true, it is evident,* and similar expressions.

> It seems *that Robert has lost all his money.*
> It is true *that genius does not always bring happiness with it.*
> It is evident *that Andrews tells the truth.*

This construction is really the same as that in § 436, 2.

438. The uses of *shall* and *will*, *should* and *would*, in **indirect discourse** are the same as in the **direct**,[48] with the following exception:—

When the first person with *shall* or *should* in direct discourse becomes the second or third person in the indirect, *shall* or *should* is retained.

> DIRECT: You say, "*I shall* die."
> INDIRECT: You say that *you shall* die.
>
> DIRECT: You said, "*I shall* die."
> INDIRECT: You said that *you should* die.
>
> DIRECT: He says, "*I shall* die."
> INDIRECT: He says that *he shall* die.
>
> DIRECT: He said, "*I shall* die."
> INDIRECT: He said that *he should* die.

The reason for the retention of *shall* or *should* is that, in such cases, the second or third person of the indirect discourse represents the first person of the direct.

The change from *shall* (after *says*) to *should* (after *said*) is a mere change of tense, according to the rule in § 434.

NOTE. The general principle is, to retain in the indirect discourse the auxiliary of the direct, simply changing the tense if necessary (§ 434). This principle of course covers the use of *you* or *he shall* or *should* to represent *I shall* or *should*. There is, however, one important exception to the general principle: when its application would result in the use of *I will* or *I would* to express mere futurity, *I shall* or *I should* is employed. Thus, John says to Charles, "If you fall overboard, *you will* drown"; but Charles, reporting this, must say, "John tells me that, if I fall overboard, *I shall* [NOT *will*] drown." The general rule, then, may be stated as follows: The indirect discourse retains the auxiliary of the direct (with a change in tense, if necessary), unless such retention makes *will* or *would* express simple futurity in the first person,—in that case, *shall* or *should* is used.

439. The following sentences illustrate the correct use of *shall* and *will*, *should* and *would*, in the indirect discourse:—

1. He writes me that he believes *he shall* be at Eton till the middle of November.—GRAY. [Direct: I shall be at Eton.]

2. He that would pass the latter part of his life with honor and decency, must, while he is young, consider that *he shall* one day be old.—JOHNSON. [Direct: I shall one day be old.]

3. Could he but reduce the Aztec capital, he felt that *he should* be safe.—PRESCOTT. [Direct: I shall be safe.]

4. Plantagenet took it into his head that *he should* like to learn to play at bowls.—DISRAELI. [Direct: I should like.]

5. He answered that *he should* be very proud of hoisting his flag under Sir John's command.—SOUTHEY. [Direct: I shall (*or* should) be, etc.]

6. He knew that if he applied himself in earnest to the work of reformation, *he should* raise every bad passion in arms against him.—MACAULAY. [Direct: If I apply myself ..., I shall raise, etc.]

7. He was pleased to say that *he should* like to have the author in his service.—CARLYLE. [Direct: I should like.]

8. Mr. Tristram at last declared that *he* was overcome with fatigue, and *should* be happy to sit down.—Henry James. [Direct: I should be happy.]

9. She vowed that unless he made a great match, *she should* never die easy.—Thackeray. [Direct: Unless you make a great match, I shall never die easy.]

10. You think now *I shall* get into a scrape at home. You think *I shall* scream and plunge and spoil everything.—George Eliot. [Direct: She will get into a scrape, etc.]

11. You in a manner impose upon them the necessity of being silent, by declaring that *you will* be so yourself.—Cowper. [Determination: I will be silent.]

12. He [Swift] tells them that *he will* run away and leave them, if they do not instantly make a provision for him.—Jeffrey. [Threat: I will run away.]

13. The king declared that *he would* not reprieve her for one day.—Mackintosh. [Direct: I will not.]

14. Horace declares that *he would* not for all the world get into a boat with a man who had divulged the Eleusinian mysteries.—Cowper. [Direct: I would not.]

15. I called up Sirboko, and told him, if *he would* liberate this one man to please me, *he should* be no loser.—Speke. [Direct: If you will liberate, etc., you shall be no loser.]

16. We concluded that, if we did not come at some water in ten days' time, *we would* return.—De Foe. [Direct: If we do not, etc., we will return.]

17. With a theatrical gesture and the remark that *I should* see, he opened some cages and released half a dozen cats.—W. J. Locke.

[Direct: You shall see.]

IX. INDIRECT QUESTIONS

440. A question expressed in the form actually used in asking it is called a direct question.

>What is your name?
>"What is your name?" he asked.

The direct form may be retained when the question is quoted or reported, as in the second example above. Often, however, a question is quoted or reported, not in the direct form, but in the form of a **subordinate clause**: as,—

>He asked *what my name was*.

Such a clause is called an **indirect question**.

441. An indirect question expresses the substance of a direct question in the form of a subordinate clause.

Indirect questions depend on verbs or other expressions of *asking, doubting, thinking, perceiving,* and the like.

>Franklin asked *where the difficulty lay*. [Direct question: "Where does the difficulty lie?"]
>The sergeant wondered *how he should escape*. [Direct question: "How shall I escape?"]
>I have not decided *which train I shall take*. [Direct question: "Which train shall I take?"]

442. Both **direct** and **indirect questions** may be introduced (1) by the interrogative pronouns *who, which, what*; (2) by the interrogative adverbs *when, where, whence, whither, how, why.*

Indirect questions may be introduced by the subordinate conjunctions *whether* (*whether ... or*) and *if*.

The use of **tenses** in indirect questions is the same as in the indirect discourse (§ 434).

> The constable inquired *whether* (or *if*) *I lived in Casterbridge.*
> [His question was: Do you live in Casterbridge?]
> Your father wishes to know *if you have been playing truant.*
> [Direct question: Have you been playing truant?]
> I considered *whether I should apply to Kent or to Arnold.*
> [Direct question: Shall I apply to Kent or to Arnold?]

443. Indirect questions are usually noun clauses. They may be used in various noun constructions: (1) as **object** of some verb of **asking** or the like, (2) as **subject**, (3) as **predicate nominative**, (4) as **appositive**, (5) as **object** of a preposition.

> The skipper asked *what had become of the cook.* [Object.]
> He was asked *what his profession was.* [Retained object after the passive (§§ 253, 389).]
> *How we could escape* was a difficult question. [Subject.]
> The problem was *how they should find food.* [Predicate nominative.]
> The question *who was to blame* has never been settled. [Apposition with *question*.]
> They all felt great perplexity as to *what they should do.* [Object of a preposition.]

An indirect question may be an adverbial clause.

They were uncertain *what course they should take*. [The clause modifies *uncertain*.]

Edmund was in doubt *where he should spend the night*. [The clause modifies the adjective phrase *in doubt*.]

444. Since the pronouns *who, which,* and *what* may be either interrogative or relative, an indirect question may closely resemble a relative clause. These two constructions, however, are sharply distinguished. A relative clause always **asserts** something. An indirect question, on the contrary, has an **interrogative** sense which may be seen by turning the question into the direct form.

The sailor *who saved the child* is a Portuguese. [The clause *who saved the child* is a relative clause, for it makes a distinct assertion about the sailor,—namely, that he saved the child. *Who* is a relative pronoun and *sailor* is its antecedent.]

{I asked | I do not know | It is still a question | It is doubtful} *who saved the child*. [Here the clause *who saved the child* makes no assertion. On the contrary, it expresses a question which may easily be put in a direct form with an interrogation point: "Who saved the child?" *Who* is an interrogative pronoun. It has no antecedent.]

The following examples further illustrate the difference between these two constructions:—

1. I foresee the course *which he will take*. [Relative clause.]
I foresee *which course he will take*. [Indirect question.]
2. I heard *what he said*. [Relative clause. *What* = "that which."]

I wondered *what he said*. [Indirect question. *What* is an interrogative pronoun.]

3. This is the man *who brought the news*. [Relative clause.]

The king asked *who brought the news*. [Indirect question.]

4. Here is a paper *which you must sign*. [Relative clause.]

The clerk will tell you *which paper you must sign*. [Indirect question.]

NOTE. In such a sentence as "Tom knows *who saved the child*," the indirect question may at first appear to be a relative clause with an omitted antecedent (*the man*, or *the person*). If, however, we insert such an antecedent ("Tom knows *the man* who saved the child"), the meaning is completely changed. In the original sentence, it is stated that Tom knows the answer to the question, "Who saved the child?" In the new form of the sentence, it is stated that Tom is acquainted with a certain person, and to this is added an assertion about this person in the form of a relative clause.

445. An indirect question is sometimes expressed by means of an interrogative pronoun or adverb followed by an infinitive.

Whom to choose is a serious question. [Direct question: Whom shall we choose?]

John asked *what to do*. [John's question was: What shall I do?]

I know *where to go*. [Direct question: Where shall I go?]

Tell me *when to strike the bell*.

I was at a loss *how to reply*.

I am in doubt *how to begin this essay*.

In the first four examples the italicized phrase is used as a noun (either as subject or object). In the fifth, the phrase *how to reply* is adverbial, modifying the adjective phrase *at a loss*.

446. The subjunctive was formerly common in indirect questions, and is still occasionally used after *if* or *whether*.

I doubt if it *be* true.

Elton questioned whether the project *were* wise.

447. The rule for *shall* (*should*) and *will* (*would*) in indirect questions is, to retain the auxiliary used in the direct question, merely changing the tense (*shall* to *should*; *will* to *would*) when necessary (§ 442).

I. Mere Futurity

1. Direct: What *shall I* do?
   Indirect: I wonder what *I shall* do.
   You ask me what *you shall* do.
   He asks me what *he shall* do.
   I wondered what *I should* do.
   You asked me what *you should* do.
   He asked me what *he should* do.
2. Direct: *Shall you* lose your position?
   Indirect: {I ask | He asks} you if *you shall* lose your position.
   {I asked | He asked} you if *you should* lose your position.
3. Direct: *Will Charles* lose his position?
   Indirect: I ask if *Charles will* lose his position.
   {I | You | Tom} asked if *Charles would* lose his position.

II. Volition

4. Direct: *Will you* help me?
   Indirect: You ask if *I will* help you.
   He asks if *I will* help him.
   You asked if *I would* help you.
   He asked if *I would* help him.

{I asked him | You asked him | Tom asked him} if *he would* {help me. | help you. | help him.}

NOTE. There is a single exception to the rule in § 447. When, in changing from a direct to an indirect question, the third person with *will* or *would* becomes the first, *shall* or *should* is substituted unless volition is expressed. Thus, John says to Thomas, "*Will Charles* die of his wound?" Charles, reporting John's question, says, "John asked Thomas whether *I should* die of my wound." Compare § 438, note.

ANALYSIS

CHAPTER I
THE STRUCTURE OF SENTENCES

448. Analysis is a Greek word which means "the act of dissolving or breaking up." In grammar it is applied to the separation of a sentence into its constituent parts, or **elements**. To dissect a sentence in this way is to **analyze** it.

The elements which make up a **sentence** are: (1) the **simple subject**; (2) the **simple predicate**; (3) **modifiers**; (4) the **complements**,—direct object, predicate objective, predicate adjective, predicate nominative; and (5) the so-called **independent elements**,—the interjection, the vocative (or nominative of direct address), the exclamatory nominative, and various parenthetical expressions (§ 501).

449. The absolute essentials for a sentence are a **substantive as subject** and a **verb as predicate** (§ 35). By combining these two indispensable elements, in various ways, with **modifiers** and **complements**, the sentence may be extended to any length desired. Indeed, the sole limits are the constructive skill of the writer and the hearer's ability to follow the thought without losing the thread.

In the present chapter, we shall consider how sentences are built up, or constructed. Our starting point in this study will be the **simple sentence**.

SIMPLE SENTENCES

450. The following statement is a **simple sentence**, for it contains but **one subject** and **one predicate** (§ 46):—

> The polar bear | lives in the Arctic regions.

The framework or skeleton of this simple sentence consists of the subject noun *bear* (the simple subject) and the predicate verb *lives* (the simple predicate). To make the **complete subject**, *bear* takes as **modifiers** the two adjectives *the* and *polar*; to make the **complete predicate**, *lives* takes as **modifier** the adverbial phrase *in the Arctic regions*.

By attaching another simple subject to *bear* we make a **compound subject**. Similarly, we make a **compound predicate** by adding another verb (§ 38).

> The polar *bear* and the *walrus* | *live* and *thrive* in the Arctic regions.

The compound subject is *bear and walrus*; the compound predicate is *live and thrive*. Both verbs are modified by the adverbial phrase *in the Arctic regions*. The sentence itself is still a simple sentence.

In each of the following simple sentences either the subject or the predicate or both are compound:—

> Games and carols closed the busy day.—ROGERS.
> The stars leap forth, and tremble, and retire before the advancing moon.—GEORGE MEREDITH.
> Madame Defarge knitted with nimble fingers and steady eyebrows, and saw nothing.—DICKENS.
> Work or worry had left its traces upon his thin, yellow face.—DOYLE.

Crows flutter about the towers and perch on every weathercock.—IRVING.

He gained the door to the landing, pulled it open, and rushed forth.—LYTTON.

Countrymen, butchers, drovers, hawkers, boys, thieves, idlers, and vagabonds of every low grade, were mingled together in a dense mass.—DICKENS.

There stood the broad-wheeled wains and the antique plows and the harrows.—LONGFELLOW.

Both Augustus and Peters joined with him in his design and insisted upon its immediately being carried into effect.—POE.

Women and children, from garrets alike and cellars, through infinite London, look down or look up with loving eyes upon our gay ribbons and our martial laurels.—DE QUINCEY.

COMPOUND SENTENCES

451. If we attach another simple sentence to that in § 450, the result is a **compound sentence**.

The polar bear | lives in the Arctic regions, ‖ but ‖ it | sometimes reaches temperate latitudes.

This is manifestly a **compound sentence**, for it consists of two **coördinate clauses**, joined by the conjunction *but* (§ 46).

The framework of the second clause consists of the subject *it* and the simple predicate *reaches*. To make the complete predicate, the verb *reaches* takes not only a modifier (the adverb *sometimes*), but a **complement**,—the direct object *latitudes*, which completes the meaning of the verb. This noun is itself modified by the adjective *temperate*. Both clauses are **simple**, for each contains but one subject and one predicate.

452. Obviously, almost any number of simple sentences may be joined (with or without conjunctions) to make one compound sentence.

> The quiet August noon has come;
> A slumberous silence fills the sky;
> The fields are still, the woods are dumb,
> In glassy sleep the waters lie.—BRYANT.

States fall, arts fade, but Nature does not die.—BYRON.

The court was sitting; the case was heard; the judge had finished; and only the verdict was yet in arrear.—DE QUINCEY.

He softly blushed; he sighed; he hoped; he feared; he doubted; he sometimes yielded to the delightful idea.—THACKERAY.

A mob appeared before the window, a smart rap was heard at the door, the boys hallooed, and the maid announced Mr. Grenville.—COWPER.

His health had suffered from confinement; his high spirit had been cruelly wounded; and soon after his liberation he died of a broken heart.—MACAULAY.

COMPLEX SENTENCES

453. The simple sentence in § 450 may be made **complex** by means of a **subordinate clause** used as a **modifier** (§ 47).

The polar bear, *which lives in the Arctic regions*, sometimes reaches temperate latitudes.

The polar bear sometimes reaches temperate latitudes *when the ice drifts southward.*

In the first example, the simple subject (*bear*), besides its two adjective modifiers (*the* and *polar*), takes a third, the adjective clause *which lives in the Arctic regions* (§ 47). The sentence, then, is **complex**: the main clause is *the polar bear sometimes reaches temperate latitudes*; the subordinate clause is *which lives in the Arctic regions.*

The second sentence is also complex. The main clause is the same as in the first (*the polar bear sometimes reaches temperate latitudes*). The subordinate clause is *when the ice drifts southward*, an **adverbial modifier** of the predicate verb *reaches*.

COMPOUND AND COMPLEX CLAUSES

454. Two or more **coördinate clauses** may be joined to make one **compound clause**.

> The polar bear, *which lives in the Arctic regions and whose physical constitution is wonderfully adapted to that frigid climate*, sometimes reaches temperate latitudes.
>
> The polar bear sometimes reaches temperate latitudes *when the floes break up and when the ice drifts southward.*

In the first example, the italicized words form a **compound adjective clause**, modifying the noun *bear*. It consists of two **coördinate adjective clauses** joined by *and*. These clauses are coördinate because they are of the same **order** or **rank** in the sentence (§ 46), each being (if taken singly) an adjective modifier of the noun.

In the second example, the predicate verb *reaches* is modified by a **compound adverbial clause**, similarly made up.

455. A clause is **complex** when it contains a modifying clause.

> The polar bear, *which lives in the Arctic regions when it is at home*, sometimes reaches temperate latitudes.

Here the **adjective clause** *which lives in the Arctic regions when it is at home* is **complex**, for it contains the adverbial clause *when it is at home*, modifying the verb *lives*.

COMPOUND COMPLEX SENTENCES

456. Two or more independent complex clauses may be joined to make a **compound complex sentence**.

> The brown bear, of which there are several varieties, is common in the temperate regions of the Eastern Hemisphere; || and || the polar bear sometimes reaches temperate latitudes when the ice drifts southward.

This is a **compound complex sentence**, for it consists of two complex clauses joined by the coördinate conjunction *and*. Each of these two clauses is independent of the other, for each might stand by itself as a complex sentence.

The first complex clause contains an adjective clause, *of which there are several varieties*, modifying *bear*; the second contains an adverbial clause, *when the ice drifts southward*, modifying *reaches*.

457. A sentence consisting of two or more independent clauses is also classed as a compound complex sentence if any one of these is complex.

The brown bear is common in the temperate regions of the Eastern Hemisphere; || and || the polar bear sometimes reaches temperate latitudes when the ice drifts southward.

The brown bear, of which there are several varieties, is common in the temperate regions of the Eastern Hemisphere; || and || the polar bear sometimes reaches temperate latitudes.

Both of these are compound complex sentences. In one, the first clause is simple (§ 451) and the second is complex. In the other, the first clause is complex and the second is simple.

CHAPTER II
ANALYSIS OF SENTENCES

SIMPLE SENTENCES

458. In analyzing a **simple sentence**, we first divide it into the **complete subject** and the **complete predicate**. Then we point out the **simple subject** with its **modifiers**, and the **simple predicate** with its **modifiers** and **complement** (if there is one). If either the subject or the predicate is compound, we mention the simple subjects or predicates that are joined.

    1. The polar bear lives in the Arctic regions.

This is a simple sentence. The complete subject is *the polar bear*; the complete predicate is *lives in the Arctic regions*. The simple subject is the noun *bear*; the simple predicate is the verb *lives*. *Bear* is modified by the adjectives *the* and *polar*; *lives* is modified by the adverbial phrase *in the Arctic regions*. This phrase consists of the preposition *in*; its object, the noun *regions*; and the adjectives *the* and *Arctic*, modifying *regions*.

    2. The polar bear and the walrus live and thrive in the Arctic regions.

The complete subject is *the polar bear and the walrus*. Two simple subjects (*bear* and *walrus*) are joined by the conjunction *and* to make a compound subject, and two simple predicates (*live* and *thrive*) are joined by *and* to make a compound predicate. *Live* and *thrive* are both modified by the adverbial phrase *in the Arctic regions*.

COMPOUND SENTENCES

459. In analyzing a **compound sentence** we first divide it into its **coördinate clauses**, and then analyze each clause by itself. Thus,—

The polar bear lives in the Arctic regions, but it sometimes reaches temperate latitudes.

This is a compound sentence consisting of two coördinate clauses joined by the conjunction *but*: (1) *the polar bear lives in the Arctic regions* and (2) *it sometimes reaches temperate latitudes*. The complete subject of the first clause is *the polar bear* [and so on, as in § 458, above]. The subject of the second clause is *it*; the complete predicate is *sometimes reaches temperate latitudes*. The simple predicate is *reaches*, which is modified by the adverb *sometimes* and is completed by the direct object *latitudes*. The complement *latitudes* is modified by the adjective *temperate*.

COMPLEX SENTENCES

460. In analyzing a **complex sentence**, we first divide it into the **main clause** and the **subordinate clause**.

1. The polar bear, which lives in the Arctic regions, sometimes reaches temperate latitudes.

This is a complex sentence. The main clause is *the polar bear sometimes reaches temperate latitudes*; the subordinate clause is *which lives in the Arctic regions*. The complete subject of the sentence is *the polar bear, which lives in the Arctic regions*; the complete predicate is *sometimes reaches temperate latitudes*. The simple subject is *bear*, which is modified by the adjectives *the* and *polar* and by the adjective clause *which lives in the Arctic regions*. The simple predicate is *reaches*, which is modified by the adverb *sometimes* and completed by the direct object *latitudes*. This complement, *latitudes*, is modified by the adjective *temperate*. The subordinate clause is introduced by the relative pronoun *which*. [Then analyze the subordinate clause.]

2. The polar bear reaches temperate latitudes when the ice drifts southward.

This is a complex sentence. The main clause is *the polar bear reaches temperate latitudes*; the subordinate clause is *when the ice drifts southward*. The complete subject of the sentence is *the polar bear*; the complete predicate is *reaches temperate latitudes when the ice drifts southward*. The simple subject is *bear*, which is modified by the adjectives *the* and *polar*. The simple predicate is *reaches*, which is modified by the adverbial clause *when the ice drifts southward*, and completed by the noun *latitudes* (the direct object of *reaches*). The complement *latitudes* is modified by the adjective *temperate*. The subordinate clause is introduced by the relative adverb *when*. [Then analyze the subordinate clause.]

3. The polar bear, which lives in the Arctic regions when it is at home, sometimes reaches temperate latitudes.

This is a complex sentence. The main clause is *the polar bear sometimes reaches temperate latitudes*; the subordinate clause is *which lives in the Arctic regions when it is at home*, which is complex, since it contains the adverbial clause *when it is at home*, modifying the verb *lives*.

4. He says that the polar bear lives in the Arctic regions.

This is a complex sentence. The main clause is *he says*; the subordinate clause is *that the polar bear lives in the Arctic regions*. The subject of the sentence is *he*, the complete predicate is *says that the polar bear lives in the Arctic regions*. The simple predicate is *says*, which is completed by its direct object, the noun clause *that ... regions*, introduced by the conjunction *that*. [Then analyze the subordinate clause.]

5. That the polar bear sometimes reaches temperate latitudes is a familiar fact.

This is a complex sentence. The main clause (*is a familiar fact*) appears as a predicate only, since the subordinate clause (*that the polar bear sometimes reaches temperate latitudes*) is a noun clause used as the complete subject of the sentence. The simple predicate is *is*, which is completed by the predicate nominative *fact*. This complement is modified by the adjectives *a* and *familiar*. The subordinate clause, which is used as the complete subject, is introduced by the conjunction *that*. [Then analyze this clause.]

COMPOUND COMPLEX SENTENCES

461. In analyzing a **compound complex** sentence, we first divide it into the **independent clauses** (simple or complex) of which it consists, and then analyze each of these as if it were a sentence by itself.

See the examples in §§ 456, 457.

CHAPTER III
MODIFIERS

462. The various kinds of **modifiers** and **complements** have all been studied in preceding chapters,—each in connection with the construction which it illustrates. For purposes of analysis, however, it is necessary to consider modifiers as such and complements as such.

The topics will be taken up in the following order:—(1) modifiers,—of the subject, of the predicate; (2) complements; (3) modifiers of complements; (4) modifiers of modifiers.

463. A word or group of words that changes or modifies the meaning of another word is called a modifier (§ 19).

{Men | *Able* men | Men *of ability*} can always find employment.

{Walls | *Battlemented* walls | Walls *with battlements*} usually enclosed mediæval cities.

{Cottages | *English* cottages | Cottages *in England*} are often thatched.

The boy listened {*eagerly.* | *with eagerness.*}

I coughed {*purposely.* | *on purpose.*}

The bullet passed {*harmlessly.* | *without doing harm.*}

464. Modifiers may be attached not only to substantives and verbs, but also to adjectives and adverbs.

All modifiers of substantives are called **adjective modifiers**; all modifiers of verbs, adjectives, and adverbs are called **adverbial modifiers**.

NOTE. The terms **adjective modifier** and **adjective** are not synonymous. All adjectives are adjective modifiers, but all adjective modifiers are not adjectives. Thus, in "Henry's skates are rusty," the possessive noun *Henry's* is an adjective modifier, since it limits the noun *skates* as an adjective might do.

465. A group of words used as a modifier may be either a **phrase** or a **clause** (§§ 40–46).

{*Able* men | Men *of ability* | Men *who have ability*} can always find employment.

I spoke {*thoughtlessly.* | *without thinking.* | *before I thought.*}

A phrase or a clause used as an adjective modifier is called an adjective phrase or clause.

A phrase or a clause used as an adverbial modifier is called an adverbial phrase or clause.

Adjective and adverbial clauses are always **subordinate**, because they are used as parts of speech (§ 46).

MODIFIERS OF THE SUBJECT

466. Any substantive in the sentence may take an adjective modifier, but **modifiers of the subject** are particularly important.

The simple subject may be modified by (1) an **adjective**, an **adjective phrase**, or an **adjective clause**; (2) a **participle**; (3) an **infinitive**; (4) a **possessive**; (5) an **appositive**.

I. ADJECTIVES, ADJECTIVE PHRASES, ADJECTIVE CLAUSES

467. The simple subject may be modified by an **adjective**, an **adjective phrase**, or an **adjective clause**.

{*Ivory* trinkets | Trinkets *of ivory* | Trinkets *which were carved from ivory*} lay scattered about.

{*Treeless* spots | Spots *without trees* | Spots *where no trees grew*} were plainly visible.

In each of these groups of sentences, the subject of the first sentence is modified by an **adjective**, that of the second by an **adjective phrase**, that of the third by an **adjective clause**.

Most adjective phrases are **prepositional** (§ 42), as in the examples.

468. An **adjective clause** may be introduced by a **relative pronoun** or a **relative adverb**. For lists, see § 377.

I. Relative Pronouns

The architect *who designed this church* was a man of genius.

The painter *whom Ruskin oftenest mentions* is Turner.

A piece of amber *which is rubbed briskly* will attract bits of paper.

The day *that I dreaded* came at last.

The plain *through which this river flows* is marvelously fertile.

The book *from which I got this information* is always regarded as authoritative.

A friend *in whom one can trust* is a treasure beyond price.

The boys *with whom he associates* do him no good.

II. Relative Adverbs

The spot *where the Old Guard made their last stand* is marked by a bronze eagle.

The morning *when I arrived in Rome* is one of my pleasantest memories.

The year *after Ashton left home* brought fresh disaster.

The land *whence Scyld drifted in his magic boat* will never be known.

Note. A preposition and a relative pronoun may often replace a relative adverb. Thus, in the second example, *on which* might be substituted for *when*.

II. PARTICIPLES

469. The subject may be modified by a **participle** (with or without modifier or complement).

1. *Smiling*, the child shook his head.
2. My aunt, *reassured*, took up her book again.
3. The prisoner sank back *exhausted*.
4. *Exasperated* beyond endurance, the captain cut the rope.
5. John, *obeying* a sudden impulse, took to his heels.
6. *Having broken* one oar, Robert had to scull.
7. The natives, *fearing* captivity above all things, leaped into the river.
8. Albert left the room, *looking* rather sullen.

In the fourth example the participle is modified by an adverbial phrase; in the fifth and sixth, it has an object; in the seventh, it has both an object and a modifier; in the eighth, it is followed by the predicate adjective *sullen*. In analysis, the whole participial phrase (consisting of the participle and accompanying words) may be treated as an adjective phrase modifying the subject; but it is simpler to regard the participle as the modifier, and then to enumerate its modifiers, etc., separately.

Thus, in the seventh example, the simple subject *natives* is modified by the participle *fearing*, which has for a complement *captivity* (the direct object) and is modified by the adverbial phrase *above all things*.

NOTE. A participle, though a modifier of the subject, has at the same time a peculiar relation to the predicate, because it may take the place of an adverbial clause. Thus, in the seventh example, *fearing* is practically equivalent to the clause *because they feared*, which, if substituted for the participle, would of course modify the predicate verb *leaped*. This dual office of the participle comes from its twofold nature as (1) an adjective and (2) a verb. In analyzing, we treat the participle as an adjective modifier of the noun to which it belongs; but its function as a substitute for an adverbial clause is an important means of securing variety in style.

III. INFINITIVES

470. The subject may be modified by an **infinitive**.

> Eagerness *to learn* was young Lincoln's strongest passion.
> Desire *to travel* made Taylor restless.
> The wish *to succeed* prompted him to do his best.
> Ability *to write rapidly* is a valuable accomplishment.
> Howard's unwillingness *to desert a friend* cost him his life.

In the fourth example, the infinitive has an adverbial modifier (*rapidly*); and in the fifth, it has a complement, its object (*friend*). In such instances, two methods of analysis are allowable, as in the case of participial phrases (§ 469).

IV. POSSESSIVES

471. The subject may be modified by a substantive in the **possessive case**.

Such a substantive may be called a **possessive modifier**.

Napoleon's tomb is in Paris.

A *man's* house is his castle.

One's taste in reading changes as one grows older.

A *moment's* thought would have saved me.

The *squirrel's* teeth grow rapidly.

The *Indians'* camp was near the river.

His name is Alfred.

Your carriage has arrived.

In each of these examples, a substantive in the possessive case modifies the subject by limiting its meaning precisely as an adjective would do.

NOTE. An adjective phrase may often be substituted for a possessive. Thus, in the first example, instead of "*Napoleon's* tomb" one may say "the tomb *of Napoleon*" (§ 93).

V. APPOSITIVES

472. The subject may be modified by a **substantive in apposition** (§ 88, 5).

Meredith the *carpenter* lives in that house.

Herbert, our *captain*, has broken his leg.

The idol of the Aztecs, a grotesque *image*, was thrown down by the Spaniards.

Many books, both *pamphlets* and bound *volumes*, littered the table. [Here the subject (*books*) is modified by two appositives.]

Appositives often have modifiers of their own.

Thus *carpenter* is modified by the adjective *the*, *captain* by the possessive *our*, *image* by the adjectives *a* and *grotesque*.

In analyzing, the whole appositive phrase (consisting of the appositive and attached words) may be regarded as modifying the subject. It is as well, however, to treat the appositive as the modifier and then to enumerate the adjectives, etc., by which the appositive itself is modified.

473. A **noun clause** may be used as an appositive, and so may be an adjective modifier (§ 386).

> The question *whether Antonio was a citizen* was settled in the affirmative. [Here the italicized clause is used as a noun in apposition with *question*.]
>
> The statement *that water freezes* seems absurd to a native of the torrid zone. [The clause *that water freezes* is in apposition with *statement*.]

An adjective in the appositive position is often called an **appositive adjective** (§ 172). "A sword, *keen* and *bright*, flashed from the soldier's scabbard."

MODIFIERS OF THE PREDICATE

474. The **simple predicate**, being a verb or verb-phrase, can have only **adverbial modifiers**.

The simple predicate may be modified by (1) an **adverb**, an **adverbial phrase**, or an **adverbial clause**, (2) an **infinitive**, (3) an **adverbial objective**, (4) a **nominative absolute**, (5) an **indirect object**, (6) a **cognate object**.

I. ADVERB, ADVERBIAL PHRASE, ADVERBIAL CLAUSE

475. The simple predicate may be modified by an **adverb**, an **adverbial phrase**, or an **adverbial clause**.

> The landlord collects his rents {*monthly.* | *on the first of every month.* | *when the first of the month comes.*}

The old schoolhouse stands {*there.* | *at the cross-roads.* | *where the roads meet.*}

We left the hall {*early.* | *before the last speech.* | *while the last speech was being delivered.*}

In each of these groups, the simple predicate of the first sentence is modified by an adverb, that of the second by an adverbial phrase, and that of the third by an adverbial clause.

Most adverbial phrases are **prepositional** (§ 42).

Adverb	Adverbial Phrase
speedily	with speed
furiously	with fury
lately	of late
instantly	in an instant
there	in that place
rapidly	at a rapid rate
skillfully	in a skillful manner
skillfully	with skill
promptly	on the instant
to-morrow	on the morrow
unwillingly	against my will

Peculiar adverbial phrases are:—

to and fro, now and then, up and down, again and again, first and last, full speed, full tilt, hit or miss, more or less, head first, upside down, inside out, sink or swim, cash down.

476. An adverbial clause that modifies a verb may be introduced by (1) a **relative adverb**, or (2) a **subordinate conjunction**.

I. Relative Adverbs

Our colonel was always found *where the fighting was fiercest*.
When I give the signal, press the button.
Whenever I call, you refuse to see me.
Miller arrived *after the play had begun*.
Everybody listened *while the vagrant told his story*.
My uncle laughed *until the tears came*.
The prisoner has not been seen *since he made his escape*.

II. Subordinate Conjunctions

Archer resigned *because his health failed*.
I will give the address *if you will let me choose my subject*.
Brandon insisted on walking, *although the roads were dangerous*.
The child ran with all her might *lest she should be too late*.
I gave you a front seat *in order that you might hear*.
The town lies at the base of a lofty cliff *so that it is sheltered from the north wind*.

II. INFINITIVE

477. The simple predicate may be modified by an **infinitive** (§ 323).

He lay down *to rest*.
I stopped *to listen*.

> The fire continued *to burn*.
> The wind began *to subside*.
> Jack worked hard *to fell* the tree.
> Will did his best *to win* the prize.
> Kate began *to weep* bitterly.
> That draughtsman seems *to be* remarkably skilful.

The infinitive may have a complement or a modifier, as in the last four examples.

III. ADVERBIAL OBJECTIVE

478. The simple predicate may be modified by an **adverbial objective** (§ 109).

> I have waited *ages*.
> We have walked *miles*.
> Arthur practised *weeks*.

The addition of modifiers to the adverbial objective makes an adverbial phrase.

> Walter ran *the entire distance*.
> He stayed *a whole day*.
> I will forgive you *this time*.
> He came at me *full tilt*.
> The wind blew *all night*.
> Come with me *a little way*.

In the first sentence, the adverbial phrase *the entire distance* modifies the verb *ran* as an adverb would do. This phrase consists of the noun *distance* with its adjective modifiers, *the* and *entire*.

IV. NOMINATIVE ABSOLUTE

479. The simple predicate may be modified by a **nominative absolute** (§ 345).

A substantive in the **absolute construction** makes with its modifiers an adverbial phrase.

> *The ship having arrived*, we all embarked.
> We shall sail on Tuesday, *weather permitting*.
> *That done*, repair to Pompey's theatre.
> *The bridge across the chasm being only a single tree trunk*, we hesitated to attempt the passage.

In the first sentence, the adverbial absolute phrase, *the ship having arrived*, is equivalent to the adverbial prepositional phrase, *on the arrival of the ship*, and defines the time of the action expressed by the verb *embarked*.

V. INDIRECT OBJECT

480. The simple predicate may be modified by an **indirect object** (§ 105).

> He gave *me* a watch. [= He gave a watch *to me*.]
> Tom told *me* the whole story. [= Tom told the whole story *to me*.]

In these sentences, the indirect object *me*, being equivalent to a prepositional phrase, is an adverbial modifier.

> The objective of service (§ 106) is also an adverbial modifier.

VI. COGNATE OBJECT

481. The simple predicate may be modified by a **cognate object** or by a phrase containing such an object (§ 108).

> The officer looked *daggers* at me [= looked at me angrily].
> The shepherd sang a merry *song* [= sang merrily].
> The skipper laughed a scornful *laugh* [= laughed scornfully].

In the first sentence, the cognate object (*daggers*) modifies the predicate verb (*looked*) as the adverb *angrily* would do. It is therefore an adverbial modifier. In the second and third sentences the modifier of the predicate verb (*sang, laughed*) is an adverbial phrase consisting of a cognate object (*song, laugh*) with its adjective modifiers (*a merry, a scornful*).

CHAPTER IV
COMPLEMENTS

482. 1. Some verbs have a meaning that is **complete in itself**. Such a verb needs only a subject. When this has been supplied, we have a sentence, for the mere verb, without any additional word or words, is capable of being a predicate.

>Birds *fly*.
>Fishes *swim*.
>The sun *shines*.
>The moon *rose*.
>The man *scowled*.
>The girl *laughed*.
>The owls *hooted*.
>The clock *ticked*.

Verbs of this kind are sometimes called **complete verbs**, or **verbs of complete predication**.

2. Other verbs are not, by themselves, capable of serving as predicates. Thus,—

>The Indians killed ——.
>Mr. Harris makes ——.
>Tom is ——.
>The man seemed ——.

These are not sentences, for the predicate of each is unfinished. The verb requires the addition of a substantive or an adjective to complete its sense.

>The Indians killed *deer*.
>Mr. Harris makes *shoes*.
>Tom is *captain*.
>The man seemed *sorry*.

Verbs of this kind are often called **incomplete verbs**, or **verbs of incomplete predication**.

>NOTE. The meaning of the verb determines to which of these classes it belongs. Accordingly, the same verb may belong to the first class in some of its senses and to the second in others (§§ 212–215).

483. A substantive or adjective added to the predicate verb to complete its meaning is called a complement.

Complements are of four kinds,—the direct object, the predicate objective, the predicate nominative, and the predicate adjective.

In the examples in § 482, *deer* and *shoes* are **direct objects**,—the former denoting the **receiver** of the action, the latter denoting the **product**; *captain* is a **predicate nominative**, denoting the same person as the subject *Tom* (§ 88, 2); *sorry* is a predicate adjective describing the subject *man*.

Complements may, of course, be modified. If they are substantives, they may take adjective modifiers; if adjectives, they may take adverbial modifiers (§§ 464, 494).

484. For convenience, the definitions of the four kinds of complements are here repeated, with examples.

1. THE DIRECT OBJECT

485. Some verbs may be followed by a substantive denoting that which receives the action or is produced by it. These are called **transitive verbs**. All other verbs are called **intransitive**.

A substantive that completes the meaning of a transitive verb is called its direct object (§ 100).

> The direct object is often called the **object complement**, or merely the **object of the verb**.

>> Alfred has broken his *arm*.
>> Morse invented the electric *telegraph*.
>> Black foxes command a high *price*.
>> You have accomplished a *task* of great difficulty.
>> Have you lost the *dog* which your uncle gave you?
>> He asked *me* the *news*. [Two direct objects (§ 103).]

Most of these objects are modified,—*arm* by the possessive *his*; *telegraph* by *the* and *electric*; *price* by *a* and *high*; *task* by the adjective phrase *of great difficulty*; *dog* by *the* and by the adjective clause *which your uncle gave you*.

486. A noun clause may be used as the direct object of a verb (§ 386).

>> You promised *that my coat should be ready to-day*.
>> The mayor ordered *that the street should be closed for three hours*.
>> I begged *that my passport might be returned to me*.

For further examples, see §§ 407, 432, 439, 441.

2. THE PREDICATE OBJECTIVE

487. Verbs of *choosing, calling, naming, making,* and *thinking* may take two objects referring to the same person or thing.

The first of these is the direct object, and the second, which completes the sense of the predicate, is called a predicate objective (§ 104).

> The **predicate objective** is often called the **complementary object** or the **objective attribute**.

> The people have elected Chamberlain *governor*.
> Peter calls Richard my *shadow*.
> The court has appointed you the child's *guardian*.
> John thinks himself a *hero*.

488. An **adjective** may serve as a **predicate objective**. Thus,—

> I thought your decision *hasty*.
> I call that answer *impertinent*.
> The jury found the prisoner *guilty*.
> Your letter made him *joyful*.

Care should be taken not to confuse adverbs with adjectives in *-ly* serving as predicate objectives.

> You called him *sickly*. [Adjective.]
> You called him *early*. [Adverb.]

After the passive, a predicate objective becomes a **predicate nominative** (§ 489).

3. THE PREDICATE NOMINATIVE

489. A substantive standing in the predicate, but describing or defining the subject, agrees with the subject in case and is called a predicate nominative (§ 88, 2).

> A predicate nominative is often called a **subject complement** or an **attribute**.

The predicate nominative is common after *is* and other copulative verbs, and after certain transitive verbs in the passive voice.

> Chemistry is a useful *science*.
> Boston is the *capital* of Massachusetts.
> Jefferson became *President*.
> This bird is called a *flamingo*.
> Mr. Hale was appointed *secretary*.
> Albert has been chosen *captain* of the crew.
> You are a *friend* upon whom I can rely.

In most of the examples, the predicate nominative has one or more modifiers. In the first sentence, *science* is modified by the two adjectives *a* and *useful*; in the second, *capital* is modified by the adjective phrase *of Massachusetts*; in the last, *friend* is modified by the adjective clause *upon whom I can rely*.

For the distinction between the **predicate nominative** and the **direct object**, see § 102.

490. A **noun clause** may be used as a predicate nominative (§ 386).

> My plan is *that the well should be dug to-morrow*.
> His intention was *that you should remain here*.
> The result is *that he is bankrupt*.
> Ruth's fear was *that the door might be locked*.

491. An **infinitive** may be used as a predicate nominative.

>To hear is *to obey*.
>
>My hope was *to reach* the summit before dark.
>
>Their plan was *to undermine* the tower.
>
>My habit is *to rise* early.

The infinitive may have a complement or modifiers. In the second and third examples, it takes an object; in the fourth it is modified by an adverb.

4. THE PREDICATE ADJECTIVE

492. An adjective in the predicate belonging to a noun or pronoun in the subject is called a predicate adjective.

A predicate adjective completes the meaning of the predicate verb and is therefore a complement (§ 172, 3.)

Like the predicate nominative, the predicate adjective is common after copulative verbs and after certain transitive verbs in the passive voice (§§ 172, 3; 252).

>John was *angry*.
>
>My knife is growing *dull*.
>
>The task seemed very *easy*.
>
>The report proved *false* in every particular.
>
>The boat was thought *unsafe*.
>
>The cover was made perfectly *tight*.

In some of these examples, the predicate adjective has a modifier. In the third, *easy* is modified by the adverb *very*; in the fourth, *false* is modified by the adverbial phrase *in every particular*; in the last, *tight* is modified by *perfectly*.

493. An **adjective phrase** may be used as a predicate adjective. Thus,—

Richard was *out of health*. [Compare: Richard was *ill*.]
Rachel seemed *in a passion*. [Compare: seemed *angry*.]
This act is *against my interests*. [Compare: is *harmful* to me.]

The adjective phrase may consist of an infinitive with or without the preposition *about* (§ 319).

I was *about to speak*.
This house is *to let*.
I am *to sail* to-morrow.

CHAPTER V
MODIFIERS OF COMPLEMENTS AND OF MODIFIERS

COMPLEMENTS MODIFIED

494. Complements, being either substantives or adjectives, may be modified in various ways, most of which have been noted in Chapter III.

1. A **substantive** used as a **complement** may have the same kinds of modifiers that are used with the **subject** (§ 466).

2. An **adjective complement** admits only **adverbial modifiers**.

495. The following sentences illustrate the modifiers of substantive complements:—

Herbert lost *a gold* watch. [The direct object (*watch*) is modified by the adjectives *a* and *gold*.]

The duke built towers *of marble*. [The direct object (*towers*) is modified by the adjective phrase *of marble*.]

My father built *the* house *in which I was born*. [The direct object (*house*) is modified by the adjective *the* and the adjective clause *in which I was born*.]

I saw *a* man *running* across the field. [The direct object (*man*) is modified by the adjective *a* and the participle *running*.]

You have forfeited *your* right *to vote*. [The direct object (*right*) is modified by the possessive pronoun *your* and the infinitive *to vote*.]

I have seen *Henry's* brother. [The direct object (*brother*) is modified by the possessive noun *Henry's*.]

I must ask *my* brother, the *mayor*. [The direct object (*brother*) is modified by the possessive pronoun *my* and the appositive *mayor*.]

The guild has elected Walter *honorary* president. [The predicate objective (*president*) is modified by the adjective *honorary*.]

Her husband is *an old* soldier. [The predicate nominative (*soldier*) is modified by the adjectives *an* and *old*.]

Her sons are veterans *of the Franco-Prussian war*. [The predicate nominative (*veterans*) is modified by the adjective phrase *of the Franco-Prussian war*.]

They are rivals *in business*. [The predicate nominative (*rivals*) is modified by the adjective phrase *in business*.]

The author is Will Jewell, *who was formerly editor of "The Pioneer."* [The predicate nominative (*Will Jewell*) is modified by the adjective clause *who was formerly editor*, etc.]

Baldwin is *the* man *standing* under the tree. [The predicate nominative (*man*) is modified by the adjective *the* and the participle *standing*.]

Your chief fault is *your* inclination *to procrastinate*. [The predicate nominative (*inclination*) is modified by the possessive pronoun *your* and the infinitive *to procrastinate*.]

This man is *Gretchen's* brother. [The predicate nominative (*brother*) is modified by the possessive noun *Gretchen's*.]

The first to fall was *the* bugler, *John Wilson*. [The predicate nominative (*bugler*) is modified by the adjective *the* and the appositive *John Wilson*.]

496. Adjective clauses are very common as modifiers of substantive complements (cf. § 468).

> Have you lost the watch *that your cousin gave you*?
> This is the very spot *where the temple of Saturn stood*.
> The general issued an order *that all non-combatants should be treated well*.
> We have abundant proof *that during his stay on the Continent, Bacon did not neglect literary and scientific pursuits*.

497. An **adjective** used as a complement may be modified by an **adverb**, an **adverbial phrase**, or an **adverbial clause**.

> I am *very* sorry *for you*. [*Sorry* is modified by the adverb *very* and the adverbial phrase *for you*.]
> Charles seems {*rather* | *very* | *extremely*} angry.
> The road is rough {*in places.* | *where they are repairing it.*}
> The whole tribe appeared eager *for war*.
> He grew envious *of his successful rival*.
> Be zealous *in every righteous cause*.
> The chief's face looked dark *with passion*.
> He was selfish *beyond belief*. [The predicate adjective (*selfish*) is modified by the adverbial phrase *beyond belief*.]
> Ellen seemed desirous *that her friends should admire her*.
> The secretary appeared unwilling *to resign*. [See § 321, note.]

MODIFIERS OF OTHER MODIFIERS

498. Modifiers may themselves be modified.

The chief varieties of such modification are illustrated in the following sentences.

I. **Adjectives** or **adjective phrases** may be modified by **adverbs** or by words or groups of words used adverbially.

> A *very* old man came to the door.
> An *exceedingly* dangerous curve lay beyond the bridge.
> This *rather* odd proposal interested us.
> The quay is *miles* long. [Adverbial objective (§ 109).]
> *At least* five different amendments have been offered. [*Five* is modified by the adverbial phrase *at least*.]
> The general, *wholly* in the dark as to the enemy's intentions, ordered an advance. [The adjective phrase *in the dark* is modified by *wholly*.]
> *Quite* at his ease, John began to speak. [*At his ease* is modified by *quite*.]
> Her smile, pathetic *in its weariness*, quickly faded. [The adverbial phrase modifies *pathetic*]
> This sleeve is *a good two inches* short. [The phrase modifies *short*.]

II. **Possessive nouns** may be modified by adjectives or by possessives.

> *The poor* man's days are numbered.
> *Honest* Tom's face shone with delight.
> *The faithful* animal's head drooped.
> *My* uncle's barn is on fire.
> *John's* brother's name is Reginald.

III. **Appositives** may be modified by adjectives or by groups of words used as adjectives.

> Joe, *the old* butler, met me at the station.
> Sam, *the cunning* rascal, had stolen the oars.
> Her mother, a woman *of fashion*, sadly neglected her.
> The other, the man *at the table*, laughed rudely.
> Ferdinand Oliver, the engineer *who had charge of the construction*, proved incompetent.
> Two Englishmen, friends *whom I visited last summer*, are coming to New York in December.

IV. **Adverbs** or **adverbial phrases** may be modified by adverbs or by words or groups of words used adverbially.

> Jane plays *very* well.
> Robert spoke *almost* hopefully.
> She answered *quite* at random.
> I write to him *at least* once *a year*.

499. An adjective may be modified by an **infinitive** (§ 321).

> Unable *to move*, I suffered torments of anxiety.
> The sailors, eager *to reach* the island, plunged into the sea.
> Reluctant *to act*, but unwilling *to stand* idle, Burwell was in a pitiful state of indecision.

500. Adjective and adverbial clauses are very common as modifiers of modifiers (cf. § 496).

> Geronimo, an old chief *who bore the scars of many battles*, led the attack. [The adjective clause modifies the appositive *chief*.]

The servant, angry *because he had been rebuked*, slammed the door as he went out.

The hunter, confident *that the deer had not heard him*, took deliberate aim.

The fugitive, in a panic *lest he should be overtaken*, made frantic efforts to scale the cliff. [The adverbial clause modifies the adjective phrase *in a panic*.]

CHAPTER VI
INDEPENDENT ELEMENTS

501. A word or group of words that has no grammatical connection with the sentence in which it stands is called an independent element.

Independent elements are of four kinds,—interjections, vocatives (or nominatives by direct address), exclamatory nominatives, and parenthetical expressions.

>*Ah!* why did I undertake this task?
>
>Help arrived, *alas!* too late.
>
>You are a strange man, *Arthur*.
>
>*Mary*, come here!
>
>Poor *Charles*! I am sorry for him.
>
>*Clothes! clothes!* you are always wanting clothes.
>
>Lucky *she*! we are all envious of her prospects.

The first two sentences contain **interjections** (§ 372); the second two, **vocatives** (or nominatives by direct address) (§ 88, 3); the last three, **exclamatory nominatives** (§ 88, 4).

When the independent word has a **modifier** (as in the fifth and seventh examples), the whole phrase may be treated as an independent element.

502. A word or group of words attached to or inserted in a sentence as a mere comment, without belonging either to the subject or the predicate, is said to be parenthetical.

>The market, *indeed*, was already closed.

Peter, *to be sure*, was not very trustworthy.

The house, *at all events*, is safe.

The road is, *I admit*, very hilly.

Luttrell's method, *it must be confessed*, was a little disappointing.

Richard was not a bad fellow, *after all*.

503. In analysis, an independent element is mentioned by itself, and not as a part of the complete subject or the complete predicate.

CHAPTER VII
COMBINATIONS OF CLAUSES

504. The use of subordinate clauses as complements and modifiers, and as modifiers of complements and of modifiers, may produce sentences of great length and complicated structure.

Such sentences, if skilfully composed, are not hard to follow. Their analysis requires merely the intelligent application of a few simple principles, which have already been explained and illustrated.

505. These principles may be summed up as follows:—

I. All clauses are either **independent** or **subordinate**. A clause is subordinate if it is used as a part of speech (noun, adjective, or adverb); otherwise, it is independent (§ 46).

II. **Coördinate** means "of the same rank" in the sentence (§ 46).

1. Two or more **independent clauses** in the same sentence are manifestly coördinate.

> *The fire blazed* and *the wood crackled*. [Two declarative clauses.]
> *What is your name*, and *where were you born*? [Interrogative clauses.]
> *Sit down* and *tell me your story*. [Imperative clauses.]

2. Two or more **subordinate clauses** are coördinate *with each other* when they are used together in the same construction,—as nouns, adjectives, or adverbs.

Such a group may be regarded as forming one **compound subordinate clause**.

> The truth is, *that I have no money* and *that my friends have forsaken me*. [Noun clauses.]
>
> The Indians, *who were armed with long lances*, and *who showed great skill in using them*, made a furious attack on the cavalry. [Adjective clauses.]
>
> *When he had spoken*, but *before a vote had been taken*, a strange tumult was heard in the outer room. [Adverbial clauses.]

In the first example, we have a **compound noun clause**; in the second, a **compound adjective clause**; in the third, a **compound adverbial clause**.

3. Coördinate clauses are either joined by coördinate conjunctions (*and, or, but*, etc.), or such conjunctions may be supplied without changing the sense (§ 362).

> The good-natured old gentleman, *who was friendly to both parties*, [AND] *who did not lack courage*, AND *who hated a quarrel*, spoke his mind with complete frankness.

III. A subordinate clause may depend on another subordinate clause.

> The horse shied *when he saw the locomotive*. [The subordinate clause depends upon the independent (main) clause.]
>
> The horse shied when he saw the locomotive, *which was puffing violently*. [The second subordinate clause depends upon the first, being an adjective modifier of *locomotive*.]

In such cases, the whole group of subordinate clauses may be taken together as forming one **complex subordinate clause**.

Thus, in the second example, *when he saw the locomotive, which was puffing violently* may be regarded as a complex adverbial clause modifying *shied*, and containing an adjective clause (*which was puffing violently*).

506. From the principles summarized in § 505, it appears that—

Clauses (like sentences) may be simple, compound, or complex.

1. A **simple clause** contains but one subject and one predicate, either or both of which may be compound (§ 451).

2. A **compound clause** consists of two or more coördinate clauses (§ 454).

3. A **complex clause** consists of at least two clauses, one of which is subordinate to the other.

507. The **unit** in all combinations of clauses is clearly the **simple sentence**, which, when used as a part of a more complicated sentence, becomes a **simple clause**.

The processes used in such combinations, as we have seen, are really but two in number,—**coördination** and **subordination**.

Coördination of clauses produces compound sentences or compound clauses; subordination of one clause to another produces complex sentences or complex clauses.

508. Every sentence, however long and complicated, belongs (in structure) to one of the three classes,—**simple**, **compound**, and **complex**.

SIMPLE SENTENCES

509. A simple sentence may have a **compound subject or predicate** (or both), and may also include a number of modifiers and complements.

Obviously, then, a simple sentence need not be short. It remains **simple in structure** so long as it contains but one simple or compound subject and one simple or compound predicate. Thus,—

1. You leave Glasgow in a steamboat, go down the Clyde fourteen miles, and then come to Dumbarton Castle, a huge rock five or six hundred feet high, not connected with any other high land, and with a fortress at the top.—WEBSTER.

The length of this sentence is due partly to its compound predicate, partly to the modifier (and modifiers of the modifier) attached to the noun *Dumbarton Castle*.

2. He was little disposed to exchange his lordly repose for the insecure and agitated life of a conspirator, to be in the power of accomplices, to live in constant dread of warrants and king's messengers, nay, perhaps, to end his days on a scaffold, or to live on alms in some back street of the Hague.—MACAULAY.

This sentence is lengthened by means of a series of infinitives used as adverbial modifiers of the complement *disposed* (a participle used as an adjective). Each of these infinitives takes a complement or a modifier (or both).

3. The arbitrary measures of Charles I, the bold schemes of Strafford, and the intolerant bigotry of Laud, precipitated a collision between the opposite principles of government, and divided the whole country into Cavaliers and Roundheads.—MAY.

Both the subject and the predicate are compound. Each of the three nouns in the compound subject has modifiers. The two verbs in the compound predicate have each a complement, and the second has an adverbial modifier (a phrase).

4. Twenty of the savages now got on board and proceeded to ramble over every part of the deck and scramble about among the rigging, making themselves much at home and examining every article with great inquisitiveness.—POE.

The predicate is compound. The sentence is extended by the use of participles (*making* and *examining*), which modify the simple subject *twenty*.

5. She was tumbled early, by accident or design, into a spacious closet of good old English reading, without much selection or prohibition, and browsed at will upon that fair and wholesome pasturage.—LAMB.

6. The mermaid was still seen to glide along the waters, and mingling her voice with the sighing breeze, was often heard to sing of subterranean wonders, or to chant prophecies of future events.—SCOTT.

7. With early dawn, they were under arms, and, without waiting for the movement of the Spaniards, poured into the city and attacked them in their own quarters.—PRESCOTT.

8. Arming a desperate troop of slaves and gladiators, he overpowered the feeble guard of the domestic tranquillity of Rome, received the homage of the Senate, and, assuming the title of Augustus, precariously reigned during a tumult of twenty-eight days.—GIBBON.

NOTE. A **simple sentence with compound predicate** often differs very slightly from a **compound sentence**. Thus in examples 4–7 the insertion of a single pronoun (*they, she*) to serve as a subject for the second verb (*proceeded, browsed*, etc.) will make the sentence compound.

COMPOUND AND COMPLEX SENTENCES

510. Every sentence that is not simple must be either **compound** or **complex**.

A sentence is **compound** if it consists of two or more independent clauses; **complex**, if it consists of one independent (main) clause and one or more subordinate clauses.

511. An ordinary **compound sentence** consists of two or more coördinate simple clauses.

Such a sentence may be of great length (as in the last example below), but its structure is usually transparent.

> A cricket chirps on the hearth, | and | we are reminded of Christmas gambols long ago.—HAZLITT.
>
> The moments were numbered; | the strife was finished; | the vision was closed.—DE QUINCEY.
>
> The old king had retired to his couch that night in one of the strongest towers of the Alhambra, | but | his restless anxiety kept him from repose.—IRVING.
>
> The clock has just struck two; | the expiring taper rises and sinks in the socket; | the watchman forgets his hour in slumber; | the laborious and the happy are at rest; | and | nothing wakes but meditation, guilt, revelry, and despair.—GOLDSMITH.
>
> The present, indeed, is not a contest for distant or contingent objects; | it is not a contest for acquisition of territory; | it is not a contest for power and glory; | as little is it carried on merely for any commercial advantage, or any particular form of government; | but | it is a contest for the security, the tranquillity, and the very existence of Great Britain, connected with that of every established government and every country in Europe.—PITT.

512. A **complex sentence**, in its most elementary form, consists of one simple independent (main) clause and one simple subordinate clause.

> The gas exploded when I struck a match.
> Though he is idle, he is not lazy.

The carpenter who fell from the roof has recovered from his injuries.

Their eyes were so fatigued with the eternal dazzle and whiteness, that they lay down on their backs upon deck to relieve their sight on the blue sky.—KEATS.

The shouts of thousands, their menacing gestures, the fierce clashing of their arms, astonished and subdued the courage of Vetranio, who stood, amidst the defection of his followers, in anxious and silent suspense.—GIBBON.

513. Both compound sentences and complex sentences admit of much variety in structure, according to the nature and the relations of the clauses that compose them.

COMPOUND COMPLEX SENTENCES

514. Any or all of the coördinate clauses that make up a compound sentence may be complex. In that case, the sentence is called a compound complex sentence.

NOTE. Compound complex sentences form a special class or subdivision under the general head of compound sentences.[49]

Old Uncle Venner was just coming out of his door, with a wood-horse and saw on his shoulder; and, trudging along the street, he scrupled not to keep company with Phœbe, so far as their paths lay together; nor, in spite of his patched coat and rusty beaver, and the curious fashion of his tow-cloth trousers, could she find it in her heart to outwalk him.—HAWTHORNE.

This sentence consists of **three coördinate clauses**, each independent of the others. These are joined by the coördinate conjunctions *and*, *nor*. The first and the third clause are **simple**, but the second clause is **complex**. Hence the whole forms one **compound complex sentence**.

The complex clause consists of two clauses, the second of which is subordinate to the first. Taken as a whole, however, this complex clause is manifestly coördinate with the two simple clauses, since the three form a series joined by coördinate conjunctions.

515. Further examples of **compound complex sentences** are:—

1. The people drove out King Athamas, because he had killed his child; and he roamed about in his misery, till he came to the Oracle in Delphi.—Kingsley.

2. Society is the stage on which manners are shown; novels are their literature.—Emerson.

3. We keep no bees, but if I lived in a hive I should scarcely have more of their music.—Cowper.

4. The same river ran on as it had run on before, but the cheerful faces that had once been reflected in its stream had passed away.—Froude.

5. There are some laws and customs in this empire very peculiar; and if they were not so directly contrary to those of my own dear country, I should be tempted to say a little in their justification.—Swift.

6. Here they arrived about noon, and Joseph proposed to Adams that they should rest awhile in this delightful place.—Fielding.

7. I never saw a busier person than she seemed to be; yet it was difficult to say what she did.—C. Brontë.

8. Malaga possessed a brave and numerous garrison, and the common people were active, hardy, and resolute; but the city was rich and commercial, and under the habitual control of opulent merchants, who dreaded the ruinous consequences of a siege.—Irving.

9. The Spaniards were not to be taken by surprise; and, before the barbarian horde had come within their lines, they opened such a deadly fire from their heavy guns, supported by the musketry and crossbows, that the assailants were compelled to fall back slowly, but fearfully mangled, to their former position.—PRESCOTT.

10. Her cheeks were as pale as marble, but of a cold, unhealthy, ashen white; and my heart ached to think that they had been bleached, most probably, by bitter and continual tears.—HOOD.

11. The hawk, having in spiral motion achieved the upper flight, fell like a thunderbolt on the raven, stunned him with the blow, clutched him in his talons, folded him in his wings, and, the hawk undermost, they tumbled down like a black ball, till within a short distance from the earth.—TRELAWNY.

In this sentence *they were* is understood after *till*.

VARIETIES OF THE COMPLEX SENTENCE

516. A complex sentence may be expanded either by compounding the main clause, or by increasing the number of subordinate clauses. Both methods may be used in the same sentence.

517. The independent (main) clause of a complex sentence may be compound.

When they saw the ship, *they shouted for joy and some of them burst into tears.*

As they turned down from the knoll to rejoin their comrades, *the sun dipped and disappeared, and the woods fell instantly into the gravity and grayness of the early night.*—STEVENSON.

The eye of the young monarch kindled and his dark cheek flushed with sudden anger, as he listened to proposals so humiliating.—Prescott.

Sharpe was so hated in Scotland during his life, and his death won him so many friends, or pitying observers, that it is not easy to write of him without prejudice or favor.—A. Lang.

As has been the case with many another good fellow of his nation, *his life was tracked and his substance wasted by crowds of hungry beggars and lazy dependents.*—Thackeray.

Note that the subordinate clause depends on the compound main clause, not upon either of its members.

> Thus, in the first example, the subordinate clause (*when they saw the ship*) depends upon the compound main clause, *they shouted for joy and some of them burst into tears*. It is an adverbial modifier of both *shouted* and *burst*.

518. Though a complex sentence can have but one (simple or compound) main clause, there is, in theory, no limit to the number of subordinate clauses.

519. Subordinate clauses may be attached to the main clause (1) as **separate modifiers or complements**; (2) in a **coördinate series of clauses**, all in the same construction, and forming one **compound clause**; (3) in a series of **successively subordinate clauses**, forming one **complex clause**.

520. Two or more subordinate clauses may be attached to the main clause separately, each as a distinct modifier or complement.

> The bridge, *which had been weakened by the ice,* fell with a crash *while the locomotive was crossing it*. [The first subordinate clause is an adjective modifier of *bridge*; the second is an adverbial modifier of *fell*.]

The architect *who drew the plans* says *that the house will cost ten thousand dollars.* [The first subordinate clause is an adjective modifier of *architect*; the second is a complement, being the object of *says*.]

Isabella, *whom every incident was sufficient to dismay,* hesitated *whether she should proceed.*—H. WALPOLE.

As the boat drew nearer to the city, the coast which the traveller had just left sank behind him into one long, low, sad-colored line.—RUSKIN.

Those dangers which, in the vigor of youth, we had learned to despise, assume new terrors as we grow old.—GOLDSMITH.

When Farmer Oak smiled, the corners of his mouth spread till they were within an unimportant distance of his ears.—HARDY.

As Florian Deleal walked, one hot afternoon, he overtook by the wayside a poor aged man, and, as he seemed weary with the road, helped him on with the burden which he carried, a certain distance.—PATER.

While Joe was absent on this errand, the elder Willet and his three companions continued to smoke with profound gravity and in a deep silence, each having his eyes fixed on a huge copper boiler that was suspended over the fire.—DICKENS.

521. Two or more subordinate clauses in the same construction, forming one compound clause, may be attached to the main clause as a modifier or complement.

1. The truth was *that Leonard had overslept, that he had missed the train, and that he had failed to keep his appointment.*

2. The guide told us *that the road was impassable, that the river was in flood, and that the bridge had been swept away.*

3. Ellis, *whose pockets were empty and whose courage was at a low ebb,* stared dismally at the passing crowd.

4. *Before the battle was over and while the result was still in doubt,* the general ordered a retreat.

5. *After we had arrived at the hotel, but before we had engaged our rooms,* we received an invitation to stay at the castle.

6. My first thought was, *that all was lost, and that my only chance for executing a retreat was to sacrifice my baggage.*—DE QUINCEY.

7. The author fully convinced his readers *that they were a race of cowards and scoundrels, that nothing could save them, that they were on the point of being enslaved by their enemies, and that they richly deserved their fate.*—MACAULAY.

In the first and second examples, three coördinate noun clauses are joined to make one compound clause, which is used as a complement,—as a predicate nominative in the first sentence, as the direct object of *told* in the second.

In the third example, a compound adjective clause modifies *Ellis*. In the fourth and fifth, a compound adverbial clause modifies the predicate verb (*ordered, received*). In the seventh, four *that*-clauses unite in one compound clause.

522. Two or more successively subordinate clauses, forming one complex clause, may be joined to the main clause as a modifier or complement.

In such a series, the first subordinate clause is attached directly to the main clause, the second is subordinate to the first, the third to the second, and so on in succession.

> In the course of my travels, I met a good-natured old gentleman, (*a*) *who was born in the village* (*b*) *where my parents lived* (*c*) *before they came to America.*

Here *gentleman* (a complement in the main clause) is modified by the adjective clause *who was born in the village* (*a*). *Village,* in clause *a,* is modified by the adjective clause *where my parents lived* (*b*). *Lived,* the predicate verb of clause *b,* is modified by the adverbial clause *before they came to America* (*c*).

Thus it appears that *a* is subordinate to the main clause, and that *b,* in turn, is subordinate to *a,* and *c* to *b.* In other words, the three clauses (*a, b, c*) are united to make one complex clause,—*who was born in the village where my parents lived before they came to America.* This clause, taken as a whole, serves as an adjective modifier describing *gentleman.*

523. Further examples of the **successive subordination** of one clause to another may be seen in the following sentences:—

> I have passed my latter years in this city, *where I am frequently seen in public places, though there are not above half-a-dozen of my select friends that know me.*—ADDISON.

> In this manner they advanced by moonlight *till they came within view of the two towering rocks that form a kind of portal to the valley, at the extremity of which rose the vast ruins of Istakar.*—BECKFORD.

> The young fellow uttered this with an accent and a look so perfectly in tune to a feeling heart, *that I instantly made a vow I would give him a four-and-twenty sous piece, when I got to*

Marseilles.—STERNE. [The conjunction *that* is omitted before *I would* (§ 388).]

Three years had scarcely elapsed *before the sons of Constantine seemed impatient to convince mankind that they were incapable of contenting themselves with the dominions which they were unqualified to govern.*—GIBBON.

Mr. Lewis sent me an account of Dr. Arbuthnot's illness, *which is a very sensible affliction to me, who, by living so long out of the world, have lost that hardness of heart contracted by years and general conversation.*—SWIFT.

> NOTE. The method of forming complex clauses by successive subordination, if overworked, produces long, straggling, shapeless sentences, as in the following example from Borrow:—"I scouted the idea that Slingsby would have stolen this blacksmith's gear; for I had the highest opinion of his honesty, *which* opinion I still retain at the present day, *which* is upwards of twenty years from the time of *which* I am speaking, during the whole of *which* period I have neither seen the poor fellow nor received any intelligence of him." A famous instance of the use of this structure for comic effect is "The House that Jack Built."

SPECIAL COMPLICATIONS

524. The processes of **coördination and subordination** (§§ 514–523) may be so utilized in one and the same sentence as to produce a very complicated structure.

Examples of such sentences are given below, for reference (§§ 525–526). Their structure, however elaborate, is always either **complex** or **compound complex**.

I. IN COMPLEX SENTENCES

525. The following sentences are complex. They contain either compound or complex clauses, or both.

1. They preferred the silver with which they were familiar, and which they were constantly passing about from hand to hand, to the gold which they had never before seen, and with the value of which they were unacquainted.—MACAULAY.

The main clause of this complex sentence is *they preferred the silver to the gold*. To this are separately attached (§ 520) two adjective clauses, both **compound**: (1) *with which ... hand*, modifying *silver*; (2) *which they had ... unacquainted*, modifying *gold*.

2. All London crowded to shout and laugh round the gibbet where hung the rotting remains of a prince who had made England the dread of the world, who had been the chief founder of her maritime greatness and of her colonial empire, who had conquered Scotland and Ireland, who had humbled Holland and Spain.—MACAULAY.

The sentence is **complex**. The main clause is *all London crowded to shout and laugh round the gibbet*. The rest of the sentence (*where ... Spain*) forms one long complex adjective clause, modifying *gibbet*. In this complex clause, the first clause (*where ... prince*) has dependent on it a compound adjective clause (modifying *prince*), made up of four coördinate clauses, each beginning with *who*. The subordination of this compound clause to that which precedes (*where ... prince*) produces the long complex subordinate clause *where ... Spain*.

3. As we cannot at present get Mr. Joseph out of the inn, we shall leave him in it, and carry our reader on after Parson Adams, who, his mind being perfectly at ease, fell into a contemplation on a passage in Æschylus, which entertained him for three miles together, without suffering him once to reflect on his fellow-traveller.—FIELDING.

In this **complex sentence**, two subordinate clauses are separately attached to the main clause: (1) the adverbial clause *as ... inn*; (2) the adjective clause *who ... fellow-traveller*. This latter clause is complex, since it contains the adjective clause *which ... fellow-traveller*, dependent on *who ... Æschylus*, and modifying *passage*.

4. As I sit by my window this summer afternoon, hawks are circling about my clearing; the tantivy of wild pigeons, flying by twos and threes athwart my view, or perching restlessly on the white pine boughs behind my house, gives a voice to the air; a fishhawk dimples the glassy surface of the pond and brings up a fish; a mink steals out of the marsh before my door and seizes a frog by the shore; the sedge is bending under the weight of the reed-birds flitting hither and hither; and for the last half hour I have heard the rattle of railroad cars, now dying away and then revving like the beat of a partridge, conveying travellers from Boston to the country.—THOREAU.

This sentence is **complex**. Its main clause is compound, consisting of a series of six coördinate simple clauses. The whole of this long compound main clause is modified by the adverbial clause with which the sentence begins (*as ... afternoon*).

5. That they had sprung from obscurity, that they had acquired great wealth, that they exhibited it insolently, that they spent it extravagantly, that they raised the price of everything in their neighborhood, from fresh eggs to rotten boroughs; that their liveries outshone those of dukes, that their coaches were finer than that of the Lord Mayor, that the examples of their large and ill-governed households corrupted half the servants in the country; that some of them, with all their magnificence, could not catch the tone of good society, but in spite of the stud and the crowd of menials, of the plate and the Dresden china, of the venison and the Burgundy, were still low men,—these were things which excited, both in the class

from which they had sprung, and in that into which they attempted to force themselves, that bitter aversion which is the effect of mingled envy and contempt.—MACAULAY.

> This **complex sentence**, though very long, is perfectly easy to follow. It begins with a long compound noun clause (consisting of nine coördinate *that*-clauses). This would be the subject of the main predicate verb *were*, but for the fact that the pronoun *these* is inserted to act as the subject (referring back to the compound noun clause and summing it up in a single word). To the complement *things* is attached the adjective clause *which excited ... contempt*. This clause is complex, for it contains three adjective clauses, (1) *from which they had sprung* (modifying *class*), (2) *into which ... themselves* (modifying *that*), and (3) *which is ... contempt* (modifying *aversion*). All three are separately attached to the clause on which they depend, *which excited that bitter aversion*. Thus all that portion of the sentence which follows *things* forms one complex clause, modifying that noun.

6. That I may avoid the imputation of throwing out, even privately, any loose, random imputations against the public conduct of a gentleman for whom I once entertained a very warm affection, and whose abilities I regard with the greatest admiration, I will put down, distinctly and articulately, some of the matters of objection which I feel to his late doctrines and proceedings, trusting that I shall be able to demonstrate to the friends whose good opinion I would still cultivate, that not levity, nor caprice, nor less defensible motives, but that very grave reasons, influence my judgment.—BURKE.

> This is a fine example of a long, but well-constructed **complex sentence**. The main clause is *I will put down, distinctly and articulately, some of the matters of objection*. Upon this simple clause, everything else in the sentence depends in one way or another.

II. IN COMPOUND COMPLEX SENTENCES

526. Any complex sentence, however elaborate, may be used as one of the **coördinate complex clauses** that make up a **compound complex**

sentence.

1. While the king was treated at this rude rate, Cromwell, with his army, was in Scotland, obstructing the motions that were making in his favor; but on the approach of the Scots, who were much superior in number, he was forced to retire towards Dunbar, where his ships and provisions lay.—BURNET.

In this **compound complex sentence**, both coördinate clauses are complex. In each, the main clause has two subordinate clauses attached to it separately (§ 520).

2. They had seen me cut the cables, and thought my design was only to let the ships run adrift, or fall foul on each other; but when they perceived the whole fleet moving in order, and saw me pulling at the end, they set up such a scream of grief and despair as it is almost impossible to describe or conceive.—SWIFT.

In this **compound complex sentence**, both of the two coördinate clauses are complex. The first contains the noun clause [*that*] *my design ... each other*, used as the object of *thought*. The second contains two subordinate clauses, separately attached to the main clause (*they set ... despair*). For the infinitive *cut*, see § 322. The infinitive *to let* is used as a predicate nominative (§ 491); it has as its object the infinitive clause *the ships ... each other*, containing two infinitives, *run* and *fall* (§ 325).

3. While things went on quietly, while there was no opposition, while everything was given by the favor of a small ruling junto, Fox had a decided advantage over Pitt; but when dangerous times came, when Europe was convulsed with war, when Parliament was broken up into factions, when the public mind was violently excited, the favorite of the people rose to supreme power.—MACAULAY.

This **compound complex sentence** consists of two complex clauses, joined by the coördinate conjunction *but*. In each of these, the subordinate clause is compound (§ 521), consisting of several coördinate adverbial clauses introduced by relative adverbs (*while* in the first, *when* in the second).

4. The clear and agreeable language of his despatches had early attracted the notice of his employers; and before the Peace of Breda he had, at the request of Arlington, published a pamphlet on the war, of which nothing is now known, except that it had some vogue at the time, and that Charles, not a contemptible judge, pronounced it to be very well written.—MACAULAY.

In this **compound complex sentence**, the first coördinate clause is simple, the second is complex. In the second, the adjective clause *of which nothing is known* has dependent on it the group of words *except ... well written,* consisting of the preposition *except* and its object (the compound noun clause, *that ... time, and that ... well written*). This group serves as an adjective modifier of the noun *nothing.* The whole passage *of which ... well written* forms a complex adjective clause, modifying *pamphlet. It to be very well written* is a complement, being an infinitive clause used as the object of *pronounced* (§ 325).

CHAPTER VIII
ELLIPTICAL SENTENCES

527. Good usage does not demand that all sentences shall be absolutely complete. It often allows (and sometimes requires) the omission of words that, though necessary to the construction, are so easily supplied by the mind that it would be mere waste of time to utter them.

528. The omission of a word or words necessary to the grammatical completeness of a clause or sentence is called ellipsis.

A clause or sentence that shows ellipsis is said to be elliptical.

>   **Ellipsis** is a Greek word meaning "omission."

In the following examples the omitted words are supplied in brackets.

>   [I] thank you.
>   [I] pray do not [you] move.
>   [You] pass me that book.
>   Her hair is light, her eyes [are] dark blue.
>   Some of the strangers spoke French, others [spoke] Spanish.
>   Some of the patriots were armed with old flintlocks, others [were armed] with swords, still others [were armed] with pitchforks.
>   When [he was] a youth, he travelled in the East.
>   Though [he is] timid, he is no coward.
>   They were amused, though [they were] somewhat vexed.
>   While [we were] drifting downstream, we grounded on a sand bar.
>   If [it is] possible, send me word to-night.

You shall have the money this week, if [it is] necessary.

They marched slowly as if [they were] worn out.

Why [are] these tears?

Why [are you] so dejected?

He was ten years of age, his brother [was] eight [years of age].

I have more confidence in James than [I have] in Edmund.

Mary is younger than George [is young].

Tom likes you better than [he likes] me.

You like him better than I do [like him].

I like him better than Charles does [like him].

This racket is not so heavy as that [is heavy].

You are not so old as I [am old].

Peace [be] to his memory!

This is the only pencil [that] I have.

Is that the boy [whom] you hired yesterday?

They say [that] you are going to Europe soon.

529. The examples in § 528 show that most cases of ellipsis fall under two heads:

1. To avoid repetition, words are often omitted in one part of the sentence when they occur in another part.

2. Pronouns, the conjunction *that*, and some forms of the verb *is*, are often omitted when they are readily supplied.

Under the second head come (1) the ellipsis of the subject (*thou* or *you*) in imperative sentences (§ 268), (2) that of relative pronouns in the objective case (§ 151), (3) that of *is, are*, etc. (with the subject pronoun) in subordinate clauses introduced by *when, though, if,* and the like (§§ 397, 399, 417).

NOTE. The so-called "telegraphic style" omits *I* with any verb or with all verbs. It should be confined to telegrams, where space is money.

530. Adverbs indicating direction (like *forward*, *back*) are often used without a verb in imperative sentences.

> *Forward*, brave companions!
> *Down* on your knees!
> *Up*, guards, and at them!

NOTE. In older English, the omission of the verb of motion was common, even in sentences not imperative, as in the following examples from *Julius Cæsar*:—"We'll along ourselves, and meet them"; "Shall we on, and not depend on you?"

531. The ellipsis of the subordinate conjunction *that* is very common, especially in indirect discourse (§§ 388, 433).

> I know [*that*] you are my friend.
> Jack said [*that*] the boat had sunk.
> He told me [*that*] he was sorry.

532. Many constructions, originally elliptical, have become established idioms in which no ellipsis is felt. In such cases it is usually better to take the sentence as it stands, and not to supply the omitted words.

> Thus, in "He eats *as if he were famished*" the italicized words are properly treated as a subordinate clause modifying *eats* and introduced by the compound conjunction *as if*. Yet in strictness this construction is an ellipsis for "He eats as [*he would eat*] if he were famished."

533. Various ellipses are illustrated in the following sentences:—

> 1. Although in a friendly country, they marched always as if in a land of enemies.

2. The aspect of the country was as wild and dreary as the climate.

3. Do not serious and earnest men discuss Hamlet as they would Cromwell or Lincoln?—LOWELL.

4. Not so with the others.

5. Though rather shy and distrustful of this new acquaintance, Rip complied with his usual alacrity.

6. Arras was famed for its rich tapestries, Brussels for its carpets, Cambrai for its fine cambric, Lisle for its thread and the fabrics woven from it.

7. Every day brings its task, which, if neglected, is doubled on the morrow.

8. It is not easy to recover an art when once lost.

9. I wish you would go down with me to Newstead.

10. The men are all soldiers, and war and the chase their sole occupation.

11. While in this state of irresolution, she was startled by a low knock.

12. The house was tall, the skylight small and dirty, the day blind with fog.

13. I little thought you would have deserted me.

14. He is the best Oriental scholar I know.

15. Cromwell was evidently laying, though in an irregular manner, the foundations of an admirable system.

16. He was a foot taller than I.

17. This concerns you rather than me.

18. My father loved Sir Rowland as his soul.

Printed by BoD in Norderstedt, Germany